AMERICAN ECONOMIC PRE·EMINENCE

AMERICAN ECONOMIC PRE·EMINENCE
Goals for the 1990s

ANTHONY HARRIGAN
WILLIAM R. HAWKINS

USIC EDUCATIONAL FOUNDATION
WASHINGTON, D.C.

Copyright © 1989 by United States Industrial Council Educational Foundation, Washington, D.C.

All rights reserved. No part of this book may be reproduced in any manner without the prior written permission of the publisher, except in the case of brief quotations used in critical articles and reviews.

The analyses, conclusions and opinions expressed are those of the authors, and not necessarily those of the Foundation, its officers, directors, or others associated with, or funding, its work.

Inquiries and book orders should be addressed to U.S. Industrial Council Educational Foundation, 220 National Press Building, Washington, D.C. 20045, 202.662.8755.

First printing 1989.
Library of Congress Catalogue Number 88-051556
ISBN 0-944468-01-2

Cover design by Patrick Maddox
Printing by Impressions, Ltd., Gaithersburg, Md.

Also by the Authors

Putting America First:
A Conservative Trade Alternative

Contents

INTRODUCTION i

I CHALLENGE AND CRISIS: 1
THE AMERICAN ECONOMY IN THE 1980s

A Question of Will 1
The Illusion of Invulnerability 1
Lobbyists and Globalism 4
A Different World 5
Measuring Weakness 6
The Need to be Shocked 7

II THE WORLD-WIDE STRUGGLE FOR WEALTH AND POWER 9

The Free Trade Myth 9
Utopian Dreams 11
Mercantilism 11
The American Tradition 12
Economic Nationalism 14
The Technology Factor 15
A Record of Decline 17
Thrift and Duty Suffer 18

III FINANCIAL CONSTRAINTS ON U.S. POWER PROJECTION 21

The Federal Deficit 21
Deficits and Defense 22
Bases and Blackmail 23
Military Pensions 24
Defense Burden Sharing 25
The Foreign Aid Drain 27

IV GLOBAL MARKETS, NATIONAL INTERESTS 31

Foreign Tax Exemptions 31
The Global Investor 32
Deficits and Global Control 32
Foreign Financial Power 38
Offshore Production 40

V INTERNATIONAL TRADE AND INDUSTRIAL POLICIES	43
Trade and Reality	45
The Smoot-Hawley Affair	48
The Japanese Trade Situation	51
An International, Not a Global, Economy	51
Japan's National Goals	53
Country Specific Retaliation	54
Dollar Devaluation	55
Money and Power	59
VI THE POLITICAL ECONOMY OF NATIONAL POWER	63
The Military-Industrial Base	63
Economic Mobilization	65
Trade with the Soviets	68
NSC and CEA Changes	73
VII THE POLITICAL ECONOMY OF NATIONAL WEALTH	75
Strategic Industry	75
Critical Service Industries	77
Takeovers and Business Organization	79
Orderly Markets	83
Lending Institutions	84
Insurance Issues	86
Private Pension Plans	87
VIII RESOURCES: THE NEED FOR SECURITY AND INDEPENDENCE	91
Energy Independence	91
Coal and Minerals	93
Resource-based States	95
Electric Power	98
Acid Rain	101

IX	**OBSOLETE LABOR ORGANIZATIONS**	105
	Labor Unions and the Economy	105
	Labor Law Reform	108
	The Minimum Wage	110
	Unions Growing Desperate	111
	Mandated Benefits	112
X	**AMERICA'S HERITAGE:**	115
	THE FOUNDATION ON WHICH TO REBUILD	
	Social Issues	115
	The Battle Over Western Civilization	116
	The Need to Limit Immigration	119
XI	**RESURGENCE OR DECLINE: AMERICA IN THE 1990S**	121
	NOTES	127
	SELECTED BIBLIOGRAPHY	133
	INDEX	135

Introduction

This volume touches on a limited number of issues but it is an indicator of the proper approach to problem-solving and policy-making recommended by the U.S. Business and Industrial Council (USBIC) and its affiliated Educational Foundation. The USBIC is a non-partisan business association that has dealt with public policy issues for more than half a century. This set of general guidelines on various topics is not constructed with any sense of infallibility. Rather, it presents a way of looking at the world and a set of values upon which to base responses to the challenges that face the United States. It proceeds from basic American political principles and a realistic appraisal of national and international trends.

The United States is in the midst of a many-sided economic crisis caused by its unrealistic assessment of the domestic and international situations and an unwillingness to live within its means. Neither one of the two major political parties has faced up to the nature of the crisis or has fully addressed the challenge confronting the nation. Yet the four years ahead must be used in a bold, constructive way to solve the problems involved in the crisis.

The symptoms include the following: massive fiscal and trade deficits; borrowing on a colossal scale to finance domestic consumption; a pattern of international giveaways incompatible with America's diminished financial resources; deindustrialization and loss of competitiveness; a dangerous reliance on imports that make the American economy vulnerable to foreign "shocks" that are beyond its control; growing social problems with an economic underclass that can no longer look forward to industrial employment due to the shift of factory jobs overseas; a weakening of America's technological preeminence because of inadequate investment in research and development; political developments, such as the anti-nuclear movement, that prevent economic growth; a seriously weakened dollar that makes possible the buyout of American companies by foreign interests at firesale prices; a lack of savings and capital formation needed to support economic expansion; a weakened strategic industrial base on which to support national defense; overextended alliance and collective defense commitments that exceed the nation's military capabilities; an illusion of international harmony and cooperation in the midst of brutal economic competition between nations; coercive unionism that undermines economic performance; an unfounded euphoria about change in the Soviet Union and a matching neglect of the consequences to U.S. security from a modernized Soviet economy; a growing dependence on unreliable foreign energy sources; short-sighted and dangerous moves to lift restrictions on the export of strategic, high-technology equipment to hostile governments including those of the Soviet bloc; an irresponsible Congress that spends beyond the country's means and which yearly devises new methods for avoiding accountability; a staggering rate of immigration by unskilled aliens which imposes unacceptable burdens on taxpayers for education, health and welfare programs; a lack of awareness of serious regional problems in the United States that threaten to depopulate vital areas; inadequate efforts to find affordable, long-term solutions to the crisis in agriculture; a dangerously-weakened financial system plagued by bad loans; an excessive public tolerance for groups and movements hostile to American values and institutions, and thus hostile to programs for America's recovery; a seriously-weakened shipbuilding industry and merchant marine; a scandalous threat from foreign influence and lobbying on Congress, government agencies and prestigious think tanks; a shocking erosion of ethics in all sectors of American society; arrogant media monopolies that seek to become an unconstitutional fourth branch of government; the undermining of the moral and social order by drugs and pornography; a lack of government concern for family-owned and independent business; economic destabilization caused by corporate raiders, market manipulators and irresponsible speculators; and, excessive U.S. interference in foreign conflicts that are remote from this hemisphere and that do not threaten American interests, stemming from a mistaken notion that the U.S. is obligated to solve all the problems of the rest of the world rather than its own.

INTRODUCTION

This catalogue of problems and threats facing the United States is by no means complete. However, it indicates the scope of the crisis which the nation confronts, and with which the leadership of the country must being immediately to deal. There is no time to lose. Failure to address these problems will imperil the United States and threaten its future survival as a free and independent society. These problems are corroding domestic life and leaving America exposed, ineffective and vulnerable. These problems threaten to fragment American society, destroy its economic base and cause it to fall before the power of more disciplined and determined nations.

Ironically, the United States has the human and material resources needed to deal with these problems; the country should not be suffering from them at all. But a lack of realistic leadership and a decline in the commitment of the American people to growth and achievement has brought the United States to this pass. This report indicates the direction that the country must take, beginning in 1989.

Chapter I

Challenge and Crisis: The American Economy in the 1980s

A Question of Will

Anyone who promises a golden age during which everyone can simply sit back and relax is talking nonsense — dangerous nonsense, if it leads to a slackening of effort. All nations of any consequence are continually challenged. Survival depends on meeting challenges head on and overcoming them.

The real question Americans face today, as historian Walt W. Rostow has said, is whether "we remain a society with a will to survive and the energy to grapple with the problems that the flow of history places before us."[1] Dr. Rostow also quoted Samuel Johnson's dictum: "Depend upon it, sir, when a man knows he is to be hanged in a fortnight, it concentrates his mind wonderfully." That is roughly the situation of the United States as it approaches the end of the 1980s. At home and abroad, the United States is in deep trouble. It is the world's largest debtor. It cannot deal decisively with tinpot dictators. It appears to be on the verge of financing the modernization of its most dangerous adversary. In the streets of many of America's largest cities are to be seen the homeless people who have been deinstitutionalized or who for one reason or another are unable to deal with the stress of contemporary life. Economic habits are out of kilter; Americans desire to consume more than they are willing to produce, the difference being met by foreign imports financed by debt.

The Illusion of Invincibility

For decades after World War II, the American people enjoyed a level of material prosperity and national security rarely known in the history of the world. They came to believe that America existed on a plateau of comfort and strength that was destined to last forever. This was a dangerous illusion, and if the American people cannot shed it in the next few years, future historians will write of it as having been a fatal illusion.

Americans not only believed that they were invincible in terms of economic, technological and military power, but were convinced that they had the material means and the moral superiority to uplift the rest of the world. America could provide the funds for Third World development and maintain order in every region. It discounted the role of nationalism, both as a motive force in others and as a requirement for its own survival. Instead, American political leaders and intellectuals adopted an internationalist (or transnationalist) agenda based on a naive confidence in cooperation between people and governments. They neglected reality and the lessons of history, failing to grasp the tremendous strength of nationalism, particularly in economics.

Harvard Asian specialists Roy Hofheinz and Kent Calder stress this connection:

> For more than a century, nationalist sentiments . . . have been a driving force underlying Eastasian economic growth. Such sentiments, of course, have also propelled modernization elsewhere, particularly in Middle Eastern nations such as Turkey and Egypt and among "follower" European states such as Germany and Russia. But love of country has been especially important in Eastasia as a stimulus to growth and effective policy formation. This is partly because of the Eastasians' relatively strong cultural pride and their consequent humiliation at subservience to foreigners, and partly because of the abrupt and threatening circumstances in which Eastasians first encountered the industrial West.[2]

This has been called the "black ship phenomenon," in reference to the "opening" of Japan by U.S. Navy Commodore Matthew Perry's squadron of warships in 1853. Japan had been in self-imposed isolation for nearly two centuries and was thus far behind the West in science and industry. The Japanese felt humiliated by Western power and have been determined ever since to not only catch up to the West but to surpass it. This fusion of economic and national drives can be seen in the practice of many Japanese corporations in sending their executives to Shinto retreats and army boot camps for training. The purpose is to instill loyalty to both company and country and to stress that the goals for both are the same.

Americans were surprised to learn in the late 1970s that the nations of the Pacific Rim, chiefly Japan and South Korea, which had rebuilt and expanded their industrial base under the protection of American military forces, had embarked on an economic offensive that had penetrated the American economy and seized the leadership in many fields of manufacturing and technology where the U.S. had long been pre-eminent. By the time this realization had dawned, the United States had lost its lead in a number of critical industries including steel, electronics, machine tools, semiconductors, shipbuilding, robotics, and motor vehicles. Foreign imports captured from one-quarter to one-half of the American market in each of these fields. Thousands of American factories were shut down as casualties of this new trade war. Alfred E. Eckes, commissioner of the U.S. International Trade Commission, stated in August 1983 that for each $1 billion in the U.S. trade deficit, 25,000 American jobs are lost.[3]

Even in the 1970s, the United States was losing in the competition with other industrial powers to place exports in third-country markets. According to a study by James C. Abegglen and Thomas M. Hout, the industries most affected were capital equipment, chemicals, electronics, materials, fuel, food and coal. The decline in U.S. export share "has largely been replaced by Asian exports."[4]

The Northeast-Midwest "industrial heartland" became the "rust belt." Some four million high-skill, high-pay and high-productivity jobs were lost in manufacturing while American leaders congratulated themselves on creating millions of new jobs, most of which were in low-skill, low-productivity and thus low-pay service industries. A report by the Joint Economic Committee released at the end of 1986 stated that a majority of the new jobs since 1979 (58 percent) have paid less than $7,000 a year while the number of jobs paying more than $28,000 a year had actually declined.[5] The best paying jobs are the most productive jobs and these are in industry and high technology, the fields most hurt by imports. The United States is trading good industrial jobs (blue-collar and white-collar) for poor service jobs under the pressure of foreign competition. Chase Econometrics reports that service jobs pay on average 11 percent less than jobs in manufacturing. Young men have been hardest hit by the lurch away from industrial employment. Median income for males 20-24 years old (in 1984 dollars) dropped from $11,572 in 1973 to $8,072 in 1984.[6]

There has been a great deal of talk about the "record number" of new jobs created in the 1980s, but the basis for the record is the larger population base, not any significant improvement in the economy. Total employment has been expanding at the rate of 2.2 percent per year, measured from fourth quarter 1984 to second quarter 1988. This is the same rate as the average over the last twenty-five years. The principle cause of this expansion has been the increased participation of women in the workforce: two-thirds of the jobs created in the 1980s have gone to women.[7]

However, the productivity of the labor force (output per person per hour) has been nearly stagnant, increasing at only 1.5 percent annually from 1984 to 1988. This has made economic growth extremely labor intensive and has meant that, for many families, the only way to raise living standards is to add a second income to the household. Family income has increased in the 1980s, but families have had to work much harder to make this happen, with adverse consequences to the quality of family life and child rearing. This is not true economic progress.

Economists, on the basis of abstract theories drawn on classroom blackboards, proclaimed that these changes were the inevitable workings of "the market" or the "invisible hand" or simply "progress." America must accept a future based on consumer service occupations to be elevated by high technology. But as the U.S. economists shouted "hallelujah," Japanese planners at the Ministry of International Trade and Industry (MITI) smiled and turned their attention back to the real factors of production, research and market control to forge ahead in manufacturing, technology and associated services.

Lobbyists and Globalism

Profits made by foreign companies from the massive American

trade deficits of the 1980s were quickly converted into capital to be invested in the purchase of American assets. The buying of America extended far beyond land, factories and financial assets. There was a vast increase in foreign lobbying and public relations activity in Washington. Included in this effort was the acquisition of former high-ranking and influential members of Congress and the Executive branch by firms representing foreign interests. Also of concern was the purchase of influence through large donations to prestigious think tanks, particularly "conservative" policy research organizations. This lobbyist-publicist-analyst complex helped to sell the American people on the notion of a new international economic order, a "global economy" in which America must expect to see a shift in economic power overseas and increased domestic dependency on foreign corporations and banks.

However, such arguments were not accompanied by any suggestion that the United States should obtain any benefits from these changes in terms of increased military burden-sharing within the alliance system, or any reduction in America's global obligations. Instead, the United States was urged to contribute even more to the process of global wealth redistribution through direct grants of money, more loans that will never be repaid, and preferential treatment for Third World products. The United States was expected to carry as large a burden as ever, meekly accepting its diminishment in the economic sphere.

A Different World

Needed now is comprehension of the very different world that exists at the end of the 1980s and the kind of global change expected in the 1990s — changes that will impact on the United States.

A basis for intelligent leadership and political action is a clear understanding that the United States no longer has the surplus wealth that it had even ten years ago. The country has run into the oldest of economic laws: resources are limited and are less than are needed to meet all of its wants. We cannot establish our domestic priorities or set a new course on foreign and defense policy if we do not fully appreciate that fact. The central fact is that the United States has been weakened and other countries strengthened as a result of changes in the international economy.

Measuring Weakness

The weakness of the U.S. economic foundation can be measured in a number of ways:

1. Lower productivity growth in the 1980s than in the 1970s: 0.4 percent yearly 1980-86 versus 0.6 percent 1970-1979 for the economy as a whole, dismal in both periods. In industry, the picture was better, since manufacturing is where high technology has made the most impact. But even here the U.S. growth rate continued to lag. Average annual percent increases in output per hour in manufacturing compare as below.[8]

	1960-1973	1973-1985	1982-1985
Japan	10.2	5.7	5.8
France	6.5	4.3	4.2
West Germany	5.8	3.8	4.7
Italy	7.2	3.7	3.8
U.K.	4.2	3.0	4.7
Canada	4.8	1.9	2.5
United States	3.3	2.2	4.1

2. The key to productivity is investment, and America has the poorest net investment rate since the end of World War II: 4.7 percent 1980-1987, well below that of other major industrial nations.

3. Higher federal spending: 22.1 percent of GNP in 1987 as against 20.5 percent in 1979.

4. The highest federal interest payments in American history: $136 billion in 1986 on a national debt of $2.2 trillion that had doubled since 1982.

5. The largest outlays for federal entitlement benefits: $400 billion in 1986.

6. A decline in investment in infrastructure by 75 percent over twenty years.

7. Foreign debts in 1987 that were three times those in 1980.

8. A foreign trade deficit that totaled $171 billion in 1987, the sixth record deficit in a row.

9. The sale of $143 billion in U.S. assets to foreigners in 1987. The United States has been selling off assets to pay for its consumption of imports, a practical definition of bankruptcy.

10. Rising oil imports while the oil-producing regions of the U.S. suffer economic depression. Oil imports are expected to reach 70

percent of domestic consumption and add $150 billion to the trade deficit by the mid-1990s. U.S. oil refineries and reserves of oil and gas are being purchased by foreign interests, further increasing America's dependence on foreign political and economic decisions.

11. The devaluation of the dollar by 50 percent 1984-1988.

12. The decline in manufacturing as a share of GNP, from 21 percent to 18 percent since 1980. In contrast, manufacturing has increased in Japan from 25 percent to 36 percent of GNP 1981-1987.

The Need to be Shocked

Former Commerce Secretary Peter O. Peterson has said that Americans ought to be shocked by the fact that "a population half the size of our own, living on a group of islands the size of California, is adding more each year to its stock of factories, houses, bridges and laboratories — in absolute terms — than we are to ours."[9] And, Japan still has $80 billion in savings left over. This enables the Japanese to buy American electronic firms, commercial real estate, wineries, tire plants, and other assets on a mammoth scale, thereby bringing more of the American economy under Japanese control and direction. Japan is also building its own assembly plants in the United States to serve as beachheads for the increased importing of manufactured goods to compete directly with American firms. There is still plenty of Japanese money left to fund public relations and lobbying activities in the United States aimed at preventing any political moves that would stop or even slow this process.

Japan believes in building a global economic network headquartered in Tokyo. This reflects their core values of order and hierarchy and their attitude of social Darwinism that long predates Darwin. Jared Taylor, who grew up in Japan and who later did business with the Japaneses as a loan officer with Manufacturers Hanover Trust, writes:

> One of Japan's important wartime objectives was the establishment of a clear hierarchy of Asian nations. The Greater East Asia Co-Prosperity Sphere was designed as a neat international hierarchy with Japan at the top. The Japanese, with their inbred sense of order, couldn't understand why the defeated nations wouldn't recognize their

own inferiority and assume tributary positions. Japanese still have a distinct feeling of superiority over the people they overran during the war, and this attitude has been strengthened by the subsequent poor economic performance of many of them.

Since the war Japan has reconquered economically what it lost militarily. In Indonesia Japanese investment is greater than all other foreign investment combined and Japanese control is increasing in the other countries of the area. Japanese have ruthlessly exploited the cheapest labor available and have exported part of their pollution problem by setting up heavy industrial complexes overseas.[10]

When Japan was defeated at the end of World War II, the Japanese bowed to their own logic and accepted it as a sign of their inferiority vis-a-vis the United States. However, now that they are on the rise again, they see this as a sign that they have regained their superiority, a fact they believe is confirmed by the inability of the United States to react to their challenge or for Americans to get their house in order.

Japan is not the only nation striving for increased wealth and power. South Korea is pumping its products into America at a rapid rate and is as clever as Japan in marketing and lobbying. The Taiwanese are in the same league. Behind them is the awakening giant of the People's Republic of China, in the midst of an industrial revolution. China is also looking at the American market as a source of profit and a base for expansion of its industrial base. In the Western hemisphere, Brazil seeks a sizeable share of the U.S. market while doing its best to exclude American goods from its own territory. Following Brazil are the other large debtor states of Latin America who have shifted in the 1980s from net importers of American goods to net exporters to the American market.

The United States is the only large, affluent country that believes in the sophistry of "free trade." While the rest of the world is largely closed to American exports, the United States is an open target for foreign industrial strategists. Steps must be taken to correct this "imbalance of opportunity" or the sphere of American enterprise will continue to shrink.

Chapter II

The Worldwide Struggle for Wealth and Power

The "Free Trade" Myth

Chalmers Johnson, a professor of Asian Studies at the University of California at Berkeley, has delineated two general systems of political economy:

> A regulatory, or market-rational, state concerns itself with the forms and procedures . . . of economic competition, but it does not concern itself with substantive matters . . . . The developmental, or plan-rational, state by contrast, has as its dominant feature precisely the setting of such substantive social and economic goals.[1]

The United States is a market-rational state. Its leaders speak in terms of "a level playing field" or "fair trade." They are not concerned with who wins or loses the global economic "game," only that it is played by a certain set of rules. Japan and virtually every other industrial state is plan-rational. Its leaders are very interested in who wins the "game" and are determined to give their "team" every advantage, fair or foul. For most nations, the very idea that international economics is nothing more than a game is anathema. They see it as just another sign of America's naivete — and a source of weakness. They know that the stakes are much too high for the competition to be taken so lightly. Thus they resort to tariffs, subsidies, cartels, tax breaks and other devices to strengthen their companies in competition with foreign rivals. The term "trade war" is much more appropriate for this kind of outlook.

American policy is based on the concept of free trade. This theory argues against nations maintaining economic diversity and independence. Instead, it presents a global division of labor in which nations specialize and become complementary, or interdependent, rather than competitive in trade. Each country only produces what it does best — its comparative advantage. David Ricardo, an early 19th century economist, conceived his classic cloth-wine model to illustrate this. This model "proved" that agricultural Portugal should not try to compete with British manufacturers of cloth but be content to only produce wine. It could then trade wine for cloth. As has often been pointed out, this economics lesson had important strategic ramifications for the continuation of England's industrial dominance. It was an attempt to convince other nations not to challenge England's industrial leadership. But, other nations soon realized that it was impossible to be a Great Power without an industrial base. Thus England soon had plenty of competitors. Free trade provided London with no answer to these challengers and England declined after 1870. By the eve of World War I, Germany and the United States, both rejecting free trade, had surpassed England in manufacturing output.

The repeated failures of free trade in the real world, despite its popularity among academic economists, led John Maynard Keynes to conclude that "We, the faculty of economists, prove to have been guilty of presumptuous error in treating as a puerile obsession what for centuries has been a prime object of practical statecraft." That object was a favorable balance of trade; the philosophy of those who pursue it is called mercantilism. Keynes further noted:

> For some two hundred years both economic theorists and practical men did not doubt that there is a peculiar advantage to a country in a favourable balance of trade. But for the last hundred years there has been a remarkable divergence of opinion. The majority of statesmen and practical men in most countries . . . have remained faithful to the ancient doctrine; whereas almost all economic theorists have held that anxiety concerning such matters is absolutely groundless.[2]

Unfortunately in the United States today, the theorists have more influence on economic policy than do the "statesmen and practical men." Thus we have a policy that is not practical and which undermines the state.

Utopian Dreams

The free trade myth has continued intellectual success in the face of real world defeats because it is based on a utopian vision of the world that many people find inviting. Ludwig von Mises, the famed libertarian economist, has given the utopian vision as follows:

> The goal of liberalism is the peaceful cooperation of all men. It aims at peace among nations too. When there is private ownership of the means of production everywhere and when laws, the tribunals and the administration treat foreigners and citizens on equal terms, it is of little importance where a country's frontiers are drawn .... War no longer pays; there is no motive for aggression. The population of every territory is free to determine to which state it wishes to belong, or whether it prefers to establish a state of its own. All nations can coexist peacefully, because no nation is concerned about the size of its state.[3]

There is scant evidence that the world has moved towards the degree of peaceful coexistence that would allow governments to lose their concern over the "size" of their state. For what is at stake in "size" is more than just geography. It is resources: population, raw materials and industrial complexes. How economic resources are allocated between nations determines both the wealth of citizens and the power of government in the world arena. Von Mises felt that governments could safely ignore the location, ownership and control of resources and productive assets. But any government that adopts such an attitude in the current unstable environment is behaving irresponsibly.

Mercantilism

The more practical, mercantilist vision is given by Friedrich List, an economic thinker who was deeply impressed by the spirit of enterprise he saw in America. Economic strength was the key to national wealth and power. Governments had a duty to adopt policies that would increase that strength. The dream of a peaceful world united by free trade should not be confused with the reality he argued. List asked:

> ... would not every sane person consider a government to be insane which, in consideration of the benefits and the reasonableness of a state of universal and perpetual peace, proposed to disband its armies, destroy its fleets and demolish its fortresses? But such a government would be doing nothing different in principle from what the popular school requires from governments when, because of the advantages which would be derivable from general free trade, it urges that they should abandon the advantages derivable from protection.[4]

It is the hallmark of mercantilism, a philosophy fundamentally different from free trade in its assumptions, to view the balance of payments and the balance and composition of trade as an aspect of the balance of power. Charles Wilson, the best of the recent historians to concentrate on mercantilism, noted that in the years since World War II the move towards a new mercantilism has accelerated, the result being the "tendency of international trade to revert to conditions which in some ways resemble those of the seventeenth century rather than those of the nineteenth."[5]

The American Tradition

"There are some who maintain that trade will regulate itself and is not to be benefitted by the encouragements or restraints of government," wrote Alexander Hamilton in 1782. But, he continued, "This is one of those wild speculative paradoxes, which have grown into credit among us, contrary to the uniform practice and sense of the most enlightened nations."[6] As the nation's first Secretary of the Treasury, Hamilton's 1791 *Report on Manufactures* has become a classic statement of economic strategy. Hamilton was not alone in his rejection of free trade theory or in his belief that power and independence required a diversified industrial economy.

The United States advanced to first place among the industrial powers behind protective tariff walls. It was a central tenet of the Republican Party after the Civil War. A hundred years after Hamilton, Iowa Congressman John A. Kasson argued that protectionism "creates a sure foundation for the maintenance of national industry, without which no nation can be independent."[7] The 20th century dawned with the United States the world's leader in industry. President Theodore Roosevelt exclaimed "Thank God I am not a free trader." He stated that American economic policy rested "on certain fixed and definite principles, the most important of these is an avowed determination to protect the interest of the American producer, be he businessman, wage-worker or farmer."[8]

Not that anyone wanted to cut the United States off from the rest of the world. The country has always sought export markets for its agricultural goods and manufacturing surplus. There has been a willingness to negotiate reciprocal trade arrangements with foreign powers and American leaders supported an active diplomatic effort to promote trade such as the "Open Door" in China. But it was one thing to push open a door for American exports and another to open a door to foreign imports. Policy could be flexible, but the objective was firm: in a world of competing nation-states, trade policy was not a matter of economic abstraction. It was an arm of foreign policy which must serve the national interest.

From 1898 to 1970, the United States ran trade surpluses every year. In the 1970s, a couple of deficit years appeared, primarily due to the hike in imported oil prices. But the country has run a trade deficit every year since 1982, and oil prices are down. The problem today is the flood of imported manufactured goods. In the past, trade was not very important to the American economy. The massive domestic market was the firm foundation of American business and industry. Trade was an indicator of economic strength, just as deficits are now a sign of economic troubles. Today, trade plays the largest role in the economy since the United States won its independence from the British Empire two centuries ago.

Secretary of State George Shultz has repeatedly praised this "new internationalism" as a sign of progress, but his own figures do not back him up. In a speech given at Massachusetts Institute of Technology in April 1988 and distributed widely by the State Department, Shultz claimed that "The most rapid economic growth in recent history occurred in the years between 1950-1973 . . . . Our markets abroad and America's per capita income grew faster in the decades of most rapid international economic integration than they have in the recent past when the growth of world trade has slowed appreciably."[9] Yet, the period 1950-1973 were years when America ran trade surpluses and was largely independent of the world economy. More recently, deficits and increased dependency on trade has slowed our growth.

Shultz might ponder why 1979 marks a change in the world economy. That is the year of the OPEC price hike and embargo. It shocked the rest of the world into realizing the dangers of economic dependency. That is why world trade is no longer expanding as it did before 1973. Only the U.S. seems to have failed to learn this lesson. America's entanglement in the world economy has been increasing and with it America's economic problems.

Economic Nationalism

Of course, there are some who do not think such concerns are important. Most are on the Left, people who we would normally expect to rejoice at the collapse of American power. But there are even some on the Right who should know better. For example, George Gilder has repeatedly denounced "nationalistic sentiments" in regard to international economic policy. He embraces the notion that "National economics are no longer nationally owned or controlled," dismissing concerns about such a development as "nationalistic fetishes."[10] Gilder thus leaves out of his framework one of the most powerful motivators of human action.

A more realistic appraisal of the benefits of mercantilist policies come from Charles P. Doran, an international relations specialist at Johns Hopkins University. He has attributed the success of the "Japanese Model" to cultural discipline, a high savings rate, government-business cooperation and "the capacity of the society to close itself off to foreign goods, thus ensuring itself a balance of payments surplus." He then goes on to state:

> Japan's giant trading companies concentrated the bulk of their operations at home; the jobs they created were Japanese jobs; the income they generated was taxed by the Japanese government.... Part of the miracle of post-war Japanese growth was attributable to the capacity of the Japanese trading company to transfer through trade profits and jobs from abroad to the home economy.[11]

There are things that the United States needs from the international economy. Raw materials, in particular the exotic minerals essential for high technology production (those mined in South Africa), come readily to mind. But the United States also needs to gain access to, use, duplicate and improve upon scientific breakthroughs wherever they occur. A great deal of work is being done by foreign governments and industries and by multinational corporations. Under a "free trade" doctrine, we may only obtain the products generated by these new technologies rather than the technology itself and the advanced production methods involved. Such a system breeds dependence and vulnerability. Policymakers need to devise strategies that use the leverage available to us as the world's largest economy and most affluent market, in coordination with our sovereign authority as a nation-state, to insure that productive industry locates within the United States. These can't be just the "hollow corporations" that some have established here which serve only as assembly plants and marketing beachheads. Gaining knowledge and production capacity is more important for the United States than this year's model or generation of finished products whose value may be fleeting.

The Technology Factor

The United States failed to understand that even the poorest nations are able to mobilize resources, often using coercive political systems, to acquire advanced technology. When combined with very low labor costs and a lack of costly environmental controls, this technology makes possible the production of goods for the U.S. market at prices far below those of American producers. The access the United States gives to foreigners who want to work in American laboratories and research facilities often leads to the transfer, sometimes even the theft, of new technologies vital to the future well-being of the American people. At the same time, the United States has yet to face up to the research and innovation campaigns conducted in rival nations on the basis of massive government investment and market support. The country has actually limited the ability of American companies to work together in joint research projects or joint applications of research under archaic "antitrust" laws better fitted to medieval fairs than to the modern world economy.

The best analysis of America's loss of industrial-technological leadership vis-a-vis Japan comes from Dr. Charles H. Ferguson of the Massachusetts Institute of Technology, a former analyst at IBM and consultant to Intel. Dr. Ferguson cites the decline of vital U.S. companies and notes that the United States "is now a worldwide importer of high-technology projects." He says that a wide spectrum of evidence suggests America's "fundamental technological decline." Japanese and Korean steel industries, he notes, "are concentrated, strategically coordinated, government-protected oligopolies." As the U.S. technological decline continues, Dr. Ferguson adds, U.S. computer producers are being forced to choose between inferior technology and subordination to Japanese companies. He warns that major U.S. companies are abandoning production and turning themselves into distributors of Japanese products. Six Japanese companies, each with annual revenues exceeding $15 billion, control 80 percent of Japanese semiconductor production. These firms are part of huge networks of businesses and industries spread across many fields. Dr. Ferguson warns that the activities of these giant Japanese combines are "furthered by government subsidies and coordinated with protectionist policies" while the "U.S. government has consistently failed to enforce intellectual property rights, open Japanese markets, obtain reciprocal access to Japanese technology and education, or represent U.S. industries."[12]

Another failure of American policy involves its use, or rather its non-use, of its scientific attaches assigned to foreign embassies and consulates. They act as administrators, much like other embassy staffers, rather than as scouts for new technology. As Arnold Kramish, a respected consultant on issues involving nuclear power and the space program, has noted, "This situation contrasts sharply with the responsibilities of foreign science attache officers, particularly the Soviet, Japanese, French and others, which have substantial specialized technical officers specifically tasked to effect technology flows from the United States."[13]

While South Korea and Taiwan are not in the same league with Japan in terms of high-tech production, they have employed the same basic strategies as the Japanese to advance their export-oriented industrial system. Dr. Paul W. Kuznits of Indiana University reports that the governments in both countries have maintained tight control over labor. He notes that in Taiwan, employees are not allowed to strike. Though there have been significant strikes recently in South Korea, this follows a long period of strict control over union activity. The Chun government has also used wage-price guidelines. Dr. Kuznits cites Japan's long history of "government administrative guidance" for business, and the use of tax incentives, credit allocations, and direct subsidies for research and development — all methods and policies well understood or recognized in America as basic to Japan's targeting strategy against American industries.[14]

A Record of Decline

The record of the United States' deterioration over the past quarter century can be seen in its steadily declining share of world GNP, from 33 percent in 1960 to 22 percent in 1980 to about 18 percent in 1987. The advances of the last 25 years cannot be compared to those of the preceding 15 years. In the immediate post-war era, when America scored extraordinary economic and technological achievements, the nation was at the zenith of wealth and power; opportunities in business and education seemed boundless; and the middle class was enormously expanded.

In the 1970s, the processes of prosperity seemed just as strong. Though the economy was plagued with recessions, "oil shocks" and inflation, real economic growth remained strong. Beneath the surface, however, the country's technological lead began to narrow. A high rate of consumption in the 1980s caused most observers to conclude that the United States was in a period of unparalleled expansion. But the expansion was only on the surface; manufacturing in U.S. strategic sectors suffered severely while manufacturing in Japan, South Korea, West Germany and other nations forged ahead.

The reality for the United States, according to Colby H. Chandler, Chairman of Eastman Kodak Company, is that the decline of manufacturing in the United States has turned the American economy into a "house of cards."[15] In the 1970s, the United States suffered severe blows that were not fully appreciated at the time. The oil embargo resulted in lasting damage and loss of national position. American wealth was transferred to the oil-producing nations of the Middle East. The oil payments deprived the United States of wealth needed to rebuild American factories and create new technologies and infrastructures. The Arab oil states used much of their new wealth to build industries that replaced U.S. exports to the Middle East, particularly in oil refining and chemicals. Also, many of the petro-dollars paid by American consumers ended up in Europe or Asia as the industrial states in these regions expanded their exports to capture this new Arab wealth.

Even more of the money was lost through bad loans to the Third World. As part of the "recycling" of petro-dollars, American banks were urged to loan huge sums to non-oil producing Third World states to help them through the economic crisis brought on by OPEC. In addition, foreign aid and grants siphoned more capital from the United States. There were two consequences to these transfers to the Third World. First, much of the money simply vanished, used for consumption or corruption, with no chance for repayment. This severely weakened the U.S. financial system. Second, some of the capital was invested to build up Third World industries in competition with American firms, to replace U.S. exports to the Third World and to penetrate the American market itself. This was followed by demands that the American market be opened up to these new rivals so money could be earned to pay back the loans. In order to save the banks from their bad loans, American industry was to be further sacrificed.

Thrift and Duty Suffer

At the same time, investment in the productive capacity of the United States began to slow. The country lacked a pro-industrial policy; basic industries were starved for capital. The inflation of the 1970s compounded the problem by introducing bad habits into the lives of citizens and the nation as a whole. Thrift lost its place as a central value. Consumer-oriented "investment" flourished. Credit purchases of durable goods like houses, automobiles and VCRs ballooned, and a horde of new retail and service companies were formed. As inflation gutted the value of savings, it became smart to borrow and spend. As a result, the savings rate fell and never recovered. It has fallen further in the 1980s despite the drop in inflation.

Other values suffered in the era of the "no-win" Vietnam War. The concept of citizen duty was undermined by the government's decision to exempt college students from the draft (or any other form of national service). The war-fighting was left to the poor and the uneducated who could not obtain draft deferments or who could not afford to run off to Canada and collect checks from home. The tolerance shown for such actions was very harmful to a democracy that depends on a strong sense of duty among its citizens.

Another byproduct of the Vietnam War was a radicalization of the intellectual elites: their considerable disaffection with traditional American values — political, moral and economic — and their unprecedent antagonism towards American national interests. More than a few intellectuals even went so far as to embrace the causes of foreign regimes hostile to the United States and to openly applaud the decline of America. The country continues to suffer from this radicalization. Many of those who used their draft deferments to pursue academic or clerical careers are now professors and ministers in major universities and churches influential in the making of policy. Certainly much of the hostility shown in elite circles towards American foreign policy and private enterprise has its roots in the late 1960s and will remain with us during the years ahead.

That the United States eventually withdrew from Southeast Asia and allowed the region to fall to the Communists has had an impact on international economics. It shattered the image of America invincibility. It is quite doubtful that OPEC would have dared to embargo oil shipments to the United States or triple the price of oil by fiat in 1973 had the U.S. not shown itself weak and indecisive in Vietnam. That America was in retreat in the world and in political turmoil at home encouraged a host of other countries to make their play.

Given the historical background to our current situation, what are Americans to do to extricate the country from its difficulties?

Certainly, the United States cannot follow the path it has taken in recent years. Failure to contain and lower the twin trade and budget deficits and to put the country on a substantially higher growth path will reduce the United States to the status of a second-class power by the end of the century, unable to meet its people's needs or to defend them in a violent world full of threats. If the country fails to act in an intelligent and decisive fashion, it could become another Argentina with a ruined currency, staggering debts, geriatric industries, outdated technology, and widespread public despair. The choices open to the United States are not easy, painless or pleasant; however, the decisions must be made.

Chapter III

Financial Constraints on U.S. Power Projection

The Federal Deficit

The first order of business is for the Executive and Legislative branches of government to agree on the goal of fiscal balance and the means to achieve it. It is the foundation stone of national renewal. If the nation's leaders cannot get their house in order, it cannot be expected that the American people as a whole will be inspired to set their private affairs in order.

The approach of the Reagan Administration was called "supply-side economics" and its aim was to grow out of our debts. Unfortunately, the actual measures introduced to achieve this goal failed in their objective. As *Business Week* has said, "The failed promise of supply side economics has left the United States with a $2.3 trillion national debt and transformed it from the world's largest creditor to its largest debtor."[1] Or as C. Fred Bergsten, director of the Institute for International Economics, put it, "The source of the 'miracle' of supply-side economics has now been revealed: foreigners supplied many of the goods and most of the money."[2] This is a situation that cannot be sustained.

The supply side idea failed for two basic reasons. First, tax cuts were concentrated on individual rates, which increased take-home pay but provided no incentives as to how that increase should be used to advance the economy. The result was that the tax cuts did far more to stimulate consumption than investment. The 1986 tax reform was particularly harmful in this respect as it brought further cuts in individual rates by shifting some $120 billion in taxes onto business investment activities. Second, though tax reform halted the overall share of GNP collected in taxes at about 19 percent, government spending continued to grow, opening a tremendous gap between revenues and expenditures.

Economic growth continued to increase tax revenues, which went from $517.1 billion in FY 1980 to $854.1 billion in FY 1987 — an increase of 65 percent. However, government spending increased faster than the economy, jumping from $590.9 billion in FY 1980 to $1,004.6 billion in FY 1987 — an increase of 70 percent. That is the exact opposite of a strategy to grow our way out of debt. To fulfill this strategy, which is the only realistic way to solve our fiscal problems, the rate of increase in government spending must be lower than the rate of economic growth so that tax revenues can catch up. That means holding the budget down and speeding the economy up. Supply side economics accomplished neither of these goals though it had pledged to do so. The idea was right, but the execution was wrong.

Lawrence A. Fox, Vice President for International Economic Affairs for the National Association of Manufacturers, has recently stated, "The United States has not improved its domestic economic performance, especially its competitiveness, vis-a-vis its principal trade competitors, Japan and Germany. Quite the opposite: the U.S. tax and national expenditure policies have accentuated the fundamental imbalance between consumption and savings/investment. The government did not stick with supply-side incentives but embraced ... consumption-oriented tax changes and deficit-spending boosts to consumption."[3]

Deficits and Defense

The negative impact of the budget deficit on the economy is well-documented. However, deficits hurt the nation in other ways. The Reagan Administration's rearmament program is being reversed under the alleged pressure of budget-cutting. Instead of reducing entitlements and welfare programs which are responsible for the large increases in government spending over the last twenty years, a liberal-dominated Congress has slashed defense in the name of a fiscal responsibility liberals have never actually believed in. The fiscal crisis has served as an excuse to shift funds from national security to the welfare state.

When defense spending accounts for only about 25 percent of the total federal budget, it cannot be the source of the budget deficit. In 1969, the last time the budget was in balance, defense spending accounted for some 40 percent of expenditures. And in 1969, defense spending was 7.8 percent of GNP. In 1987 defense spending was only 6 percent of GNP. Obviously, the spending that the government does for programs other than defense is the cause of the budget problem.

The FY 1989 budget marks the fifth year in a row that defense spending has been cut in real terms. Muscle is being cut. The Navy is forced to retire ships; the Navy and Air Force are having to disband entire air wings; and the Army is losing combat units. This is in addition to the cancellation and postponement of new weapons systems. In the end, the Reagan presidency will have the dubious honor of being second only to that of the Carter presidency for spending the lowest share of GNP on defense of any administration since before World War II.

Our foes and friends alike may become convinced that the United States is incapable of sustained defense efforts. The United States cannot afford to let that perception develop again after the disastrous record of military neglect in the 1970s. Therefore, in seeking an Executive-Legislative consensus on fiscal balance, there must also be a consensus that military security be given top priority. This is a national survival imperative.

Bases and Blackmail

This is not to say that money cannot be saved in the area of defense expenditures. One area in which cuts can and should be made is in the number of military bases maintained. The American taxpayers are saddled with the retention of hundreds of bases in the continental United States that date back before World War II. These are maintained merely as pork barrel projects, excuses to funnel federal funds to selected Congressional districts in the name of national defense. But these bases serve no military function. The Pentagon has repeatedly asked for authority to consolidate these bases in order to devote needed funds to more important projects. To date, unfortunately, Congress has declined to take effective action to close down obsolete facilities that do nothing more than provide community payrolls — a form of community welfare. The next administration must have the political courage to insist on closing bases that are no longer required for military missions.

The Executive and Congress also should decline to make political blackmail payments to countries that demand massive foreign aid in exchange for permitting U.S. bases on their territory. If anything, the United States should request that host countries underwrite the cost of building base complexes and providing defense forces that protect the host country. In addition, it should be recognized that the presence of American personnel is a tremendous source of income to the host country. In negotiations, the United States generally has more leverage than it uses. It is time to remedy that.

The Philippines in a case in point. While the Subic Bay and Clark Airfield facilities are excellent and very useful to the United States, neither the Executive branch that negotiates base agreements nor the Congress that votes the money should go along with increasingly unreasonable demands for payments. If push comes to shove and the Philippines government will not settle, then the long-range fiscal advantage as well as the military advantage lies in accepting some inconveniences now and beginning transfer to or the building of facilities on Guam or other American-controlled territories. It never pays to submit to blackmail, international or otherwise.

Military Pensions

Another defense expense which can be reduced is military pensions. The Grace Commission pointed out several years ago that military pensions are grossly excessive. They are far more generous than those in the civilian sector. The argument is often heard that the pensions are proper because servicemen put their lives on the line for their country. The truth is that the same basic pension benefits are provided to those who wear decorations for gallantry in action and to those who have never heard a shot fired in anger. This is a ridiculous system.

Of course, those who are already in the services today have contractual rights that cannot be abrogated, unreasonable though the pensions may be. However, Congress is in a position to develop a new, more reasonable and less costly pension system for those who enter the services in the future.

One feature of current military pensions that must be scrapped is the provision for retirement after 20 years of service. No corporation would agree to such a pension plan which negates the value of the investment made in a serviceman's training and enables him to start a new career with a new pension plan when he is still relatively young.

Another area where cutbacks can undoubtedly be made for former military personnel is the excessive benefits offered of access to post commissaries. Also wholly unjustified in the national interest is the existence of rules that allow former service personnel and their dependents to travel, space permitting, on military aircraft abroad as well as at home. There is no reason why the taxpayers should provide free airline service to retired military personnel.

The criticisms that apply to military pensions and benefits also apply to the excessive pension arrangements for all federal employees. Benefits must be cut now if the pension system is not to bankrupt the country in the years ahead. The worst abuses in pension benefits are those created by members of Congress for themselves. This is a continuing scandal that deserves ongoing public scrutiny.

Defense Burden-Sharing

Increased American military expenditures will be needed in order to develop and deploy new weapons systems — strategic defense and anti-satellite systems, advanced submarines and aircraft, additional aircraft carriers and armored vehicles. But the threat posed by the Soviet Union and radical Third World states will not be met unless America's allies and associates assume a proper share of the free world's defense burden.

A priority task for the Executive and Legislative branches is to end the decades-old practice whereby the United States devotes more than half of its defense budget to NATO and ensures Japan's security, including its sealanes from the Persian Gulf and Indian Ocean across the Pacific, while NATO nations and Japan devote far less of their resources to their own defense than does the United States. America devotes some 6 percent of its GNP to defense programs; the NATO countries average only about 4.5 percent and Japan 1 percent.

This spending pattern made sense when the Federal Republic of Germany and Japan were recovering from World War II and did not possess an adequate economic base. Today, however, both West Germany and Japan are economic giants and enjoy a high degree of prosperity. They also run large trade surpluses with the United States. An end to the European and Japanese free ride at America's expense is essential if the United States is to achieve fiscal balance without weakening the Western deterrent against Soviet aggression or radical terrorism.

The Soviets have built an imposing military machine. In Europe, Soviet and Warsaw Pact forces have increased their numerical superiority over U.S. and NATO forces while making significant improvements in quality. The Soviets possess a 3-1 edge in artillery, a 2.5-2 edge in tanks and tactical aircraft and a 1.5-1 edge in antitank missiles. In East Asia, the USSR has 50 combat divisions, 40 regiments of tactical aircraft and the largest concentration of the Soviet Navy. It also has such heavily armed allies in the region as Vietnam and North Korea. Within striking distance of the Persian Gulf are another 25 Soviet divisions and 900 aircraft. The U.S. Defense Department's 1987 annual report said of the Soviet threat:

> Their offensive doctrine and creation of operational maneuver groups of up to corps size imply an intention to move rapidly across Western European soil. Their growing stockpiles of ammunition and fuel are clear manifestations of their desire to sustain such a conflict.... And the Soviets have significantly improved their capabilities to launch simultaneous large-scale offensives in widely separated theaters.[4]

It is clear that the United States in an era of tight budgets cannot afford to engage all of these Soviet and communist forces at once and still guard against other threats such as Iran and Libya.

The United States should not be satisfied with merely another Japanese promise of increased defense activity over a period of years or a modest adjustment in Germany's contribution to NATO. Both of these countries are on the front line. They should assume the primary responsibility for their own defense and for the defense of areas outside Europe that affect their security. This should be a non-negotiable demand by the United States. There is no reason, for example, for America to provide naval protection to Japanese tankers sailing between the Persian Gulf and the home islands. The United States was correct to only provide convoy protection in the Gulf during the recent Iran-Iraq War to tankers flying the American flag. America should not accept the role of world policeman but should only act to achieve clearly-defined objectives.

It is often said that Japan is an ally of the United States. However, treaty requirements only involve the U.S. defense of Japan, not the Japanese defense of the United States. Several years ago, former Undersecretary of State U. Alexis Johnson pointed out that America really does not have an alliance with Japan but that Japan simply has a valuable insurance policy from the United States with very low premiums.[5] Clearly, the time has come to increase the premiums drastically.

An increase in defense efforts by allies would in no way constitute a withdrawal of the United States from its superpower role. America would still possess the greatest amount of nuclear, naval and conventional military power under the control of a single government. It would still be both the arsenal and the reserve of the free world. It is important to make this point because too often the call for allies to do more is combined with a desire, stated or unstated, for the United States to do less, for America to cut its forces as the allies expand theirs. But this would be dangerous, for the Western alliance is today outgunned by its adversaries. The purpose of a European and Japanese buildup is to strengthen the alliance against its foes, not merely shuffle around force levels that are inadequate. The goal is to better share the credit for a strong defense, not share the blame for a disastrous defeat.

The Foreign Aid Drain

While common sense compels the American people to realize that they must stop excessive spending if there is to be any hope of achieving a fiscal balance and dealing with the nation's colossal foreign debt, Congress and the Executive have continued to urge continuation of the foreign aid giveaway binge — approximately $14 billion a year. This bad habit is the result of the enduring notion that the United States as a rich nation can afford massive donations to the "underprivileged" of the world and has an obligation to run a global welfare state. The idea that the United States has billions of dollars to infuse into the World Bank and other multi-lateral lending institutions represents the same illusion. It is incredible that American officials should talk about U.S. fiscal reform and urge cuts in domestic programs and national defense while giving vast sums to other countries, most of whom are unstable, inefficient and publicly hostile to the United States and its economic and political system.

The uniquely American concept of foreign aid is deeply embedded in the political and social idealism of the immediate post-World War II period. It will not be easy to dismiss. Nevertheless, budget pressures combined with the record of foreign aid's failure seem likely to crowd it out within a few years. The slice of the pie that in past years went to the Third World is now urgently needed to bail out sick U.S. lending institutions, many themselves victims of liberal lending policies to the Third World; to rebuild the U.S. economic infrastructure that is near collapse; to pay for the mushrooming costs of medical care for an aging population; and to provide for many other domestic needs. Congress surely must acknowledge in the near future that with the budget in deficit, the only money available for foreign aid is money that the United States borrows. And the limits of borrowing, particularly borrowing from foreigners, are rapidly being realized.

The drying-up of American money will be a shock for the countries of the Third World that have lived a dependent life since being granted their independence from European rule. In many cases, American foreign aid was the result of fear that the Soviet Union would grab huge chunks of the former colonial empires. Aid was used in an attempt to buy friends in the Third World. It should be clear by now that common interests, not pay-offs, are the only secure basis for alliances.

While the Soviet Union has not abandoned its strategy of global imperialism, shown by its activities in Nicaragua, devoting vast amounts to establishing communist regimes in backward lands no longer has top priority in Moscow. The Soviets are now attending to domestic economic changes and the modernization of their own military forces, rather than concentrating on the Third World.

Unlike the United States, the USSR never did believe that spreading money around was the best way to gain influence, particularly in the American way of giving scores of countries annual sums with no strings attached. The USSR certainly never adopted the liberal notion of global wealth redistribution that has passed for foreign aid in the West. Instead, the Soviets concentrated their support on a handful of allies from which they could get direct returns in the form of mercenary troops or military bases. The strategic basis of Soviet aid is evident in the fact that though the USSR spends far less each year on total aid than does the United States, it provides far more military aid to its "friends" than does the U.S. Since the days of Stalin, the Soviets have never trusted any foreign group they could not directly control. This, of course, is the traditional form of foreign aid. When a devastating drought hit Ethiopia, a Soviet client state whose regime is kept in power by Cuban troops and East Bloc advisors, Moscow was treated to the spectacle of a massive American relief effort. As in the past, Soviet power was bailed out by American naivete.

Moscow would never stand for the type of behavior the United States has routinely endured when Third World despots cash their American checks one day and stand up to denounce American "imperialism" in the United Nations the next day. While it may be in the national interest for America to provide funds to foreign allied governments or movements from time to time, such a policy based purely on strategic considerations would be far more rational and less costly than the current approach.

The Japanese are increasing their foreign aid, but are being selective about where it goes. It is but another aspect of their overall economic strategy. Like their foreign investment pattern, they use their funds to build up areas of value to themselves. It is noteworthy that one aspirant for the American presidential nomination sought to sell to his party a similar Third World foreign aid and economic strategy. His efforts were unsuccessful. The activists and intellectuals in his party remained committed to the internationalist ideal of aid while the voting public was not interested in an issue that seemed so remote from their own bread-and-butter affairs.

Chapter IV

Global Markets, National Interest

Foreign Tax Exemptions

A failure to insist on defense burden-sharing is not the only way in which foreign countries have benefited at the expense of American citizens. The tax exemptions that the United States confers on foreign investors gives them an unfair advantage and places American investors and companies at a disadvantage. In the process, the U.S. Treasury loses an estimated $5 billion to $10 billion a year — money that would be a significant help in reducing the budget deficit.

In 1984, Congress made the mistake of repealing the 30 percent withholding tax on corporate interest paid on portfolio investments held by foreign nationals. Repeal opened the gate for foreign economic penetration of the United States. There is no reason why United States tax policy should be tilted so as to favor foreigners, while demands are voiced for imposing higher taxes on American-owned entities. In 1986, foreign nationals earned billions of dollars in interest on assets in the U.S. With markedly increased foreign acquisitions of American assets in 1987 and 1988, earnings have increased significantly. Foreigners, in fact, now earn more money from their investments in the United States than Americans earn from their investments in the rest of the world. Yet these interest earnings by foreigners are untaxed while Americans enjoy no such exemption on their interest earnings. This is one of the biggest loopholes in the tax law. It should be closed as part of the effort to balance the budget. If foreigners want to participate in the American economy and enjoy a safe shelter for their funds, at the very minimum they should be treated the same as American investors in terms of taxation.

The Global Investor

This tax loophole for foreigners is only a very small piece of a much larger problem involving the role of the global investor in the United States. H. Ross Perot, founder of Electronic Data Systems and one of America's best-known entrepreneurs, is deeply concerned about the nation's budget deficit and its connection with foreign investment in the United States: "Our country effectively does not have a national budget. We avoid facing the budget issue by passing continuous resolutions that put us deeper into debt each year.... More and more, our national debt is being funded by foreign investors." Perot warned:

> We Americans have evolved from tough, resilient people, willing to sacrifice for future generations, into a people who want to feel good now — at any price — and let the future take care of itself. Put more directly, we have become credit junkies, shooting up huge sums of borrowed money on a government and personal level — looking for another high.[1]

Former Treasury Secretary William E. Simon has observed that "the worrisome aspect of today's trade deficit is that foreign funds are borrowed, not for investment in the future, but selfishly to finance present consumption."[2]

Deficits and Global Control

America's twin deficits — budget and trade — are dangerous problems because they lead to a loss of economic sovereignty by the United States. The byproduct of the policy of heavy domestic deficit spending in the 1980s has been a determination by the administration to invite foreigners to buy into the American economy or, as some say, to buy into America, using the profits they have made from the U.S. trade deficit. These foreign funds, as Ross Perot pointed out, have financed most of the increases in the federal debt, which may reach $3 trillion by the end of the decade. In addition, there has been a great desire to attract foreign funds for investment in the private economy in an attempt to compensate for the low level of capital formation by American firms and citizens.

Free trade advocates dismiss the concept of trade deficits on the grounds that in the end accounts must balance. Dollars "lost" through trade will be regained in some form. A dollar is simply an I.O.U. which will eventually be redeemed for something of equal value. But what is this "something?" As has been mentioned before, the focus of free traders is very narrow and misses a great deal about how the world works.

Foreigners are not using their dollars to buy American products, but American assets. The situation is analogous to a consumer who charges purchases on a store credit card. The store makes a profit on both the sale and on the interest from the loan. Both provide funds with which the store can expand. It is the store that grows richer, not the consumer who simply ends up deeper in debt. Eventually, the consumer must find a way to pay off the debt, even if it means selling off his possession to raise the cash, otherwise known as bankruptcy. This is what the United States is doing when foreigners use the profits from trade to buy up property, companies, or securities. Or when they establish their own plants in the U.S. to directly compete with American firms on their own turf. Those who gain from trade gain more than money. They gain power as well.

The public is not yet aware of the extent to which foreigners are buying into America. Congress has yet to come to grips with the issue. And foreign lobbyists have bitterly resisted attempts to require disclosure of foreign ownership of assets in the United States.

The pace of foreign acquisitions has stepped up sharply. An indicator of how things have changed is the fact that Japan will soon have more manufacturing capacity for automobiles in the U.S. than will American firms. But no one knows how much — or how little — American content there is in the cars these foreign-owned plants will produce. They will use American blue-collar labor, but the decisions will be made by foreign managers, whose numbers are increasing along with foreign technicians and professionals. For example, in Tennessee, where more than thirty Japanese corporations have established operations, the Tennessee Military Institute has been bought by Japanese interests and will be converted into a high school for the children of Japanese executives. The idea is that American schools are unsuited to instruct Japanese children who are expected to return to Japan for college. This indicates not only the growth in the size of the Japanese managerial class in America, but also that this class still owes its allegiance to Japan and wishes to remain insulated from American influences. Yet, this managerial class will be making key decisions affecting the American economy in the future.

The only way to get the facts about foreign ownership in the United States and its plans for the American economy is for the appropriate Congressional committees to hold public hearings on these subjects and take testimony under oath. The new Congress should undertake this task.

Another indicator of growing foreign control of American assets is the fact that foreign investors own 46 percent of downtown Los Angeles, 25 percent of Washington D.C., 39 percent of downtown Houston and 32 percent of Minneapolis. The problem of Japanese control has become acute in Hawaii. Over the last two years, Japanese investors have bought $6.5 billion of Hawaiian real estate. This compares with their $4.5 billion investment in California and $3 billion in New York. Hiroshi Kato, economic advisor to former Japanese Prime Minister Yasuhiro Nakasone, is reported to have said that Japan would be glad to purchase more of America's assets — "Hawaii, for example."[3]

Nakasone himself caused a considerable stir in 1986 when he commented that Japan's racial homogeneity has made it a "more intelligent society" compared to that of the United States "where there are blacks, Mexicans and Puerto Ricans and the level is still low." Nakasone has also referred repeatedly to the superiority of the "Yamato race" which according to Japanese mythology united the home islands in the fifth century. Yamatoists believe that the Japanese are superior to all others and thus have an obligation to "rescue" inferior races.[4]

Attitudes like these among Japan's leaders, combined with the cold economic facts about trade and debt, lead many thoughtful Americans to ask "Is Japan colonizing America?" Certainly, as *Industry Week* noted, there is a heightened danger that American dependency on Japanese technology and Japanese goods would make it impossible to direct the American economy or mobilize production for purely national purposes in the event of a war or a depression.[5] George Gilder, an advocate of American-Japanese economic integration, has even argued that it is already too late, that American high-technology production is already completely dependent on Japanese components.[6] This may not alarm Gilder, but it should alarm every American who is concerned about the stability and long-run health of the national economy. If Gilder is correct, how could the nation's leaders have allowed such a situation to develop? If push comes to shove, the national interest of Japan will be the controlling factor in decisions made by Japanese investors, owners and managers. America will have to accept what it is given.

Contrary to what apologists for foreign ownership say, foreign "transplants" and other ostensibly American subsidiaries of foreign corporations — some of which are actually owned, wholly or in part, by foreign governments — are *not* American companies. The ultimate control rests overseas, and they are run to further the interests and the profits of the owning country. In a report on the Japanese invasion of Hawaii, *Forbes* said, "Although the U.S. flag still flies there, Hawaii looks to be well on the way to becoming an economic colony of Japan."[7] Is California, with its rich agriculture and strategic industries, the next state marked for deep Japanese penetration? The U.S. government has an obligation to look into this kind of situation during the next four years.

It is known that in recent years the Soviets endeavored to gain control of several banks in California's Silicon Valley, the heart and brains of America's high-tech industries. By controlling the finances of these innovative firms through the banks, the Soviets would have had access to files and records on the firm's research projects and would have been in a position to use leverage to gain even restricted or top secret data. The role of banks is often overlooked in the control and direction of the economy. American banks have been at the center of the world financial system for so long their dominant position has been taken for granted. Yet, American banks have lost their preeminence. Today, the ten largest banks in the world are Japanese and it is well known that Japanese banks are fully integrated into the trade and industrial strategies of Japanese mercantilism.

The United States has a committee on foreign investments that is supposed to act as a watchdog to prevent foreign control of any industry vital to national security. Unfortunately, it is virtually moribund. Authorities on the problem of foreign control report that the committee rarely meets and has never blocked a foreign investment. One critical situation is the chemical industry, certainly a strategic industry by any standard, where four of the top ten chemical companies in the United States are foreign-owned.

Effective oversight is imperative in view of the torrent of investment from abroad. At this time, no one knows the full extent or, most importantly, the character of foreign investment in the U.S. industrial base. There are important questions that must be asked by policymakers and legislators. For example, if West Germany were to move in a neutralist direction, which is a possibility given the outlook of the Social Democrats and the Greens, what would be the effect of the Bonn government's policy on key German companies operating in the United States or supplying vital components to American firms?

The difficulty of developing oversight measures is caused by the prevailing opinion that it doesn't matter where the money is coming from to finance the U.S. economy and government. Nevertheless, the source and character of the money coming into the United States has a very direct bearing on America's economic sovereignty. Billions of dollars also have poured into the United States from Latin sources in recent years; only very far-reaching investigations will determine how much of this money is tainted by drugs, terrorism or tyranny.

Getting disclosure legislation through Congress has been very difficult. In 1988, the Reagan Administration openly opposed such legislation. The author of one disclosure measure, Congressman John Bryant of Texas, has pointed out that "lobbyists for foreign interests who want to keep their identities secret — along with others who don't want to reveal the full extent to which our economic policies have caused a firesale of American assets" have worked diligently and successfully to block disclosure legislation. He said that at least one foreign-owned business directly threatened a senator that it would close down its extensive operations in his state if he actively supported the Bryant Amendment.[8] This is the very kind of blackmail that demonstrates why new laws are needed.

The objective of oversight of foreign investment in the United States is not to end all such investment, but to contain it and regulate it; to make sure that foreign investors pay their fair share of the tax burden; to insure that foreign firms are not given advantages that put their American-owned competitors at a disadvantage. The "incentives" and subsidies that many state and local governments have given to foreign transplants in their frantic attempts to outbid other communities is truly a scandal — and easily abused by the firms involved. Oversight should insure that foreign investments do not compromise American secrets or provide political leverage to those whose loyalties lie elsewhere.

Pat Choate, vice president of TRW, Inc., has said that 152 Japanese companies and government agencies have hired 113 law firms to act as their representatives in Washington. They will devote more than $100 million to lobbying this year. This amount exceeds the combined budgets of all major organizations that represent American business groups.[9] When Congress was working to pass sanctions against the Toshiba Corporation for selling classified equipment to the Soviet Union — equipment that has allowed Moscow to install super-quiet propellers on their nuclear submarines so that they can operate with much less chance of detection — Toshiba spent an estimated $60 million on a campaign in the United States to pressure Congressmen to vote against the sanctions. This campaign also included the sending out of Toshiba's American employees to confront members of Congress, like Sen. Lloyd Bentsen, at public meetings. When a foreign corporation can get Americans to side with it against the security interest of the United States, then matters have clearly gotten out of hand.

Foreign groups employ former high officials of the U.S. government and financially assist think tanks that generate research materials favorable to their interests, especially those that promote free trade. This is a lobbying scandal that has received scant attention in the media. Foreign-funded political action committees also contribute heavily to candidates of both major political parties, a practice that should be outlawed. Participation in the American political process should be limited to American citizens and not be subject to manipulation by those whose interests lie outside the United States.

Foreign Financial Power

The Executive and Legislative branches also need to take action to deal with the shift of financial power to Japan and with what *The Wall Street Journal* called the "de-Americanization" of the U.S. economy, a situation where "foreign capital now plays an extraordinary role ... [and] developments abroad now cast an enormous shadow across the U.S."[10]

Richard Drobnik, who heads the Business and Education Research Program at the University of Southern California, stated at an American Chamber of Commerce meeting in Tokyo that international financial power has shifted from the United States to Japan. "World financial policy is now set by the Bank of Japan. It is not set by the U.S. Federal Reserve at all." He added that "resentment and friction will naturally occur in the United States as Americans belatedly awake to the reality of reduced independence in managing our national economic policies."[11]

Reduced independence is reflected in the growing presence of Japanese financial institutions in the United States and their growing importance in the direction of the world economy. A decade ago, six of the ten largest banks in the world were American. Today, all ten of the largest banks are Japanese. The five largest U.S. banks have average assets of $88 billion, whereas Japan's seventh largest bank, the Industrial Bank of Japan, has assets of $161 million.[12] American banks today find themselves in direct competition with Japanese banks here in the United States. For example, in 1986, Sumitomo Bank of Japan invested $500 million in the American firm Goldman Sachs.

The Sumitomo Bank is an example of the massive integration of Japanese banks and firms. The Sumitomo Group comprises 130 companies, including banks, trading companies and two of Japan's largest insurance companies. In these combines, the banks perform the function of coordination, deciding research and production programs, division of markets and export strategies. Such cartel-like relationships are not only unknown in the United States, they are illegal under our antitrust laws.

To be sure, not everyone is unhappy with the new foreign financial environment. Walter Olson of the libertarian Manhattan Foundation is pleased with the idea of the "de-nationalization" of financial power. Olson is full of praise for those who foresee a day when financial institutions — no longer tied to their home bases by a majority of revenues, assets, stockholders, employees or managers — will themselves become as "global" in outlook as the world markets they will serve. They will cease to "belong" to any nation or to serve the interests of any particular nation. Bankers will become "men without a country."[13] This kind of ivory tower idealism won't appeal to many realistic Americans. The basic flaw in these "globalist" fantasies is that their authors believe that just because a corporation operates in many different countries, its leaders will forget their roots and their basic loyalties. But in the real world, Japanese bankers are very much aware that they are *Japanese* bankers serving the goals of Japanese business world-wide. It will be a sad day if American businessmen ever abandon their patriotism and forsake their country to pursue some conjured-up utopian mirage.

The Economist has described the Japanese objective of control, saying that the Japanese "have agreed to have a high and mighty yen, with which they will proceed to buy the world."[14] This is in reference to the policy of the U.S. Treasury to not only let the dollar fall under the pressure of the balance of payments deficit, but to encourage it to fall in the belief that this will reduce the trade deficit. This policy utterly fails to take into account that when the dollar falls, it multiplies the purchasing power of foreign currencies not only in regard to American products but also in regard to American assets. And since foreign governments have trade policies that will prevent the lower dollar from boosting U.S. exports as much as it would in an open market, the main effect of devaluation will be to increase foreign ownership of America.

The inevitability of financial and economic power becoming vested in Japan is open to question, however. Though Japan undoubtedly exerts tremendous financial power, it is, to use Frank Gibney's term, "a fragile superpower."[15] Japan remains dependent on the United States in many ways. America provides a defense shield for Japan. It also supports friendly governments in a number of other Asian lands in which Japan has substantial investments — the Philippines, Indonesia, Thailand. It controls the sealanes across which Japan's trade sails. Japan itself is an overcrowded island, with limited agricultural, fuel and raw materials sources. It has labor shortages and pollution problems. Domestic economic growth has been slow. Its entire economic system is geared to expansion in foreign markets which are subject to the sovereign control of other governments. The United States is the most important overseas market. So, America has enormous leverage over Japan. It has just failed to use the leverage to restructure the economic relationship of recent years to one more in line with American interests.

Offshore Production

Congress also needs to track more carefully American investment in offshore production. According to economist Peter F. Drucker, about one-fifth of the total capital invested by U.S. manufacturing firms is invested in facilities outside the United States. Approximately one-quarter of the goods produced in U.S.-owned plants abroad is shipped back to America for use in products then erroneously labeled "Made in the USA." In some cases, the only "work" done on the products here is the correction of production mistakes made by the cheap and low-skilled foreign labor used in the offshore operation.[16]

It is important here to distinguish between two kinds of offshore production. The first type of operation, the largest part of American overseas production, is meant to supply local markets. It is primarily the existence of foreign protectionist barriers, or strong local competition, that leads an American company to set up a factory in the market it will serve. This type of offshore production is not a problem. Its operation is not a substitute for operations in the United States. It is an attempt to reach a market that could not be reached any other way. This type of "market extension" operation is most common in developed areas such as Europe, Japan and parts of Latin America. Such production is valued at over three times that of U.S. exports. Profits repatriated from such overseas sales are a plus for the balance of payments and an important source of capital formation. Also, overseas subsidiaries of American companies are the largest single "market" for U.S. exports as these foreign subsidiaries buy equipment, components and spare parts from their parent firms back in the United States.

The second type of operations, the ones that are growing dangerous, are known as "workshop affiliates." These American-owned plants in Mexico, Taiwan, Singapore and other countries produce goods for export back to the American market. They also compete with foreign-owned workshop affiliate plants in those same countries which furnish inputs to foreign-owned plants in the United States. Peter Drucker has given the example of a Sony plant south of the border which ships goods to California for incorporation in equipment built in its San Diego factory.

Those businessmen and economic commentators who favor U.S. offshore production are best described as transnationalists. Indeed, Drucker has urged American business "to go transnational" in order to compete in the "global economy." American companies, he has said, must be prepared to engineer, design and manufacture in any part of the world.[17] It is clear, however, that advocates of transnationalism believe that U.S. companies should locate much of their manufacturing and assembly work — all designed for sale of products back in the U.S. market — in underdeveloped countries with very low labor costs. Such plants can use the same technology they would use in the United States, thus keeping output per hour roughly the same, but wages that are an order of magnitude lower.

Transnationalists, in effect, would have American companies disassociate themselves from their basic American orientation. They believe that U.S. companies should conceive of their future in global terms and operate without any special responsibilities to their American employees, to American communities where they operate or to the U.S. economy in general. That is what transnationalism means: a divorce from the traditional national business outlook and ethic.

Transnationalism should be disavowed by business and the government. Yet it is understandable, given foreign competitive pressure, why so many U.S. companies feel that they have to move their facilities offshore. The government has shown little or no interest in protecting their American operations from competition that employs cheap foreign labor, as well as subsidy and guidance from foreign states. This has led American managers to conclude that the only way for their firms to compete with foreign companies exporting to the United States is to transform themselves into foreign companies also exporting to America. Thus, another negative result of "free trade" has been to literally alienate part of the American business sector and push it out of the country.

The movement of American jobs offshore is hurtful to hundreds of American communities. It reduces tax revenues needed in the United States for schools, hospitals and other services. It destroys job opportunities for American workers and damages American ancillary operations — spare parts and components, construction and maintenance, plus a variety of business services. Obviously, the American free enterprise system won't survive if only the interests of its shareholders are protected. Home-based support — broad public support — is essential to the continuation of the free enterprise system. But that support will only be forthcoming if the public believes that free enterprise serves the common good. Thus it is in not only the national interest, but in the long-run interest of the business community, to insure that production for the American market is concentrated in the United States.

Chapter V

International Trade and Industrial Policies

According to United Nations data, in 1953 the advanced capitalist economies of Europe, Japan and the United States accounted for 72 percent of world manufacturing. By 1980 this had declined to 65 percent, with all of the lost share going to the Third World. The Communist states held steady at 23 percent during the same period.[1] Within the capitalist economies, Japan and West Germany, still recovering in 1953 from the Second World War, expanded rapidly, shifting manufacturing market shares away from the United States and various European countries (such as England). Once-strong industrial sectors in the old economic powers have become hollow shells while competing centers in these same industries have been built elsewhere, new bases from which to lead export offensives and stimulate economic growth.

Trade and industrial policies, at work in many of the fastest-growing nations for decades, have suddenly been "discovered" by their shaken rivals. Robert H. Ballance of Purdue University and Stuart Sinclair of the University of Southern California at Los Angeles have noted that there has been a "realization — albeit belated — that there are substantial portions of world industrial capacity, even outside the socialist countries, whose very existence is due to public policy decisions."[2]

The United States has been one of the last places where this discovery has been made. This is because conservatives, who are normally the most sensitive to national threats and the most supportive of economic growth, have been paralyzed by the notion that any act of government involving the economy is a sign of socialism. They have forgotten that the purpose of socialism is not the creation of wealth but its redistribution. Policy is merely a tool, to be used for purposes proper or improper. Because of their different goals, industrial policy and socialism would not only represent programs that were different in form and substance but also largely antithetical. Kevin Phillips has observed that:

> industrial policy — a neomercantilist business-government partnership — has enjoyed its most substantial successes under conservative or right-wing regimes like those found in Japan, Gaullist France, Korea, Brazil and Taiwan.... One can conclude that around the world effective, not theoretical, industrial policy fits part and parcel with what can be called *de facto* business nationalism.[3]

Phillips also warns that "insufficient conservative attention to competitiveness strategy could create . . . an opening to the left, by which antibusiness forces can trade on the public's nationalism, economic frustration and desire for action to enact more radical measures." For decades, American conservatives have surrendered the power of government and the initiative in policy formation to the Left by adopting a hands off, holier-than-thou attitude towards economics. The result has been the creation of a welfare-regulatory-fiscal environment hostile to business. Since few people have accepted the argument that government should divorce itself entirely from the economy (as if it could with a $1 trillion budget), the conservative position has simply insured that critical decisions would be made by people other than themselves.

Industrial policy does not mean the rigid bureaucracy of East bloc central planning. Economic growth depends on business savvy and the incentives provided by a system of production for profit — capitalism supported by friendly government actions. A definition as basic as that given by Chalmers Johnson would be a grand step forward:

> By industrial policy I mean the government's explicit attempt to coordinate its own multifarious activities and expenditures and to reform them using as a basic criterion the achievement of dynamic

comparative advantage for the American economy. Such an industrial policy would work on the supply-side and would be long-term in outlook. It would seek to produce aggressive investment behavior by reducing risks, providing information, promoting R&D, removing irrational antitrust barriers . . . and encouraging appropriate education and reeducation of the labor force.[4]

Johnson cites with approval Louis Mulkern's statement that "there could be no more devastating weakness for any major nation . . . than the inability to define the role of government in the economy."

Trade and Reality

America's foreign trade deficit is a national problem as great as the fiscal deficit; and the two deficits are closely related in that both represent attempts by Americans to live beyond their means, to consume more than they produce. Both are perpetuated by short-term thinking that sacrifices the future. From the trade deficit flows a wide range of problems, including deindustrialization, the export of jobs, the deterioration of major cities, fewer job opportunities for minorities, and a weakened industrial-technological base for the armed forces. It is essential that the Legislative and Executive branches of government address the trade deficit with the same seriousness as the fiscal deficit.

At the end of 1987, the trade deficit stood at a record high of $171.2 billion. Because of increased exports, achieved through the costly devaluation of the dollar, trade figures have shown a slight improvement by the middle of 1988. However, estimates still place the 1988 deficit in excess of $130 billion. This indicates how stubborn the deficit is and how inadequate current policy is. The tremendous drop of 50 percent in the value of the dollar over two and one-half years has generated an improvement in the deficit of less than 25 percent.

The failure of the United States to address the foreign trade problem is rooted in a fundamental misunderstanding of the nature of trade in the world today. While other nations have waged trade offensives to penetrate the vast U.S. market and have targeted particular American industries for economic destruction, Americans have held to unrealistic and extremely naive ideas about international economic policy. The following key points are basic to a thoroughgoing reform of U.S. trade policy:

1. A trade deficit means that profits from production are earned by foreigners who are concerned, first and foremost, with the prosperity and security of their own countries.
2. A trade deficit inhibits growth in the deficit country; by definition, a trade deficit is a subtraction from GNP.
3. The de-Americanization of the U.S. economy endangers the nation's ability and freedom to act in a crisis.
4. A trade deficit has resulted in foreign-owned plants in the U.S. that are only "hollow" corporations that engage in little more than assembly work. They are merely marketing beachheads used to circumvent expected legislation to curtail imports. Most foreign governments do not understand why the United States has not acted already to correct its trade deficit, but they eagerly exploit the delay.
5. A trade deficit leads to a shrinking industrial-technological core that serves as a base for future innovations, many of which are evolutionary or arise from interaction across disciplines. Losing a key industry now also means losing what it might become in the future.
6. The current trade deficit, 80 percent of which is due to loss of markets in manufacturing fields, means that workers are being pushed out of jobs with high productivity into service jobs with low productivity. In the long-run, the standard of living depends on productivity.
7. A trade deficit that leads to devaluation cuts American purchasing power and leads to inflation. The terms of trade shift against the United States so that people have to work harder just to stay even.
8. The historical fact is that the United States became the largest, most productive economy in the world behind high "protective" tariff walls. By 1900, the U.S. economy surged ahead of England's economy, which declined steadily from the number one position by falling for the sophistry of "free trade."
9. General free trade is not possible because other countries do not believe in it or practice it; they never have and never will. When they talk of "free trade," they only mean keeping open the U.S. market for their products, just as the United States talked of an "Open Door" in China while practicing protectionism at home.
10. Free trade allows American companies to be undersold by countries with low pay scales, oppressive domestic policies and few, if any, health, safety or environmental regulations. Competition under

these conditions rewards those with the most antisocial behavior.

11. Increased exports will be an insufficient remedy for the trade deficit because either overseas markets are closed by foreign economic policies in rival industrial states and countries, or foreign populations are unable to buy American goods due to poverty or debt in the Third World. Just as the deficit was caused by a jump in imports, it must be solved by a reduction in imports.

12. Even if trade can be brought into balance, it might not be sufficient to provide the industrial base the country needs. The United States has apparent "comparative advantage" in agriculture and services, but expanding exports in these fields will do nothing to support heavy industry and high-technology.

13. International trade, just as other forms of competition, produces winners and losers. The game is won by whoever scores the most points, not whoever plays by the "cleanest" set of rules.

14. Denying that a trade war is in progress will not prevent the United States from losing it. The war started some two decades ago, but it took a long time to erode America's initial superiority. Now the danger is upon us and little time remains to mobilize our resources to fight back.

The past failure to understand the trade situation must be recognized if sound, long-range corrective policy is to be instituted and America's industrial economy revived.

National legislators and policymakers must bear in mind that many of America's trade rivals have very different economic systems and philosophies of political economy. They have aggressive, export-oriented national industrial policies. They finance steel mills, auto plants, shipyards and other industrial operations, all of which are often owned by the government itself. Foreign laws and customs permit longer time horizons and less vulnerability to the business cycle than is true for American firms. Foreign governments work more closely with their private firms and allow them to combine, exchange labor, undertake joint projects, coordinate strategies and make other arrangements that are not currently possible under the restrictive antitrust laws of the United States. Foreign companies are often subsidized so that they can maintain operations and employment with low prices and only marginal profits from sales in order to gain or expand market share in America.

These foreign trade strategies are not "evil," but simply practical and successful. It is not "bashing" another country to recognize that it is following its own interests. This is how the world works. The United States needs to learn from the experiences of others and from the lessons of history. Only then can it determine its own interests and devise strategies to advance them.

The Smoot-Hawley Affair

In the debate over trade policy, the advocates of free trade have been hard pressed to show where their theory has ever worked. Instead, they have attempted to argue that protectionist policies do not work. Their argument has come to depend on one example: the Tariff Act of 1930, known popularly as "Smoot-Hawley" after Sen. Reed Smoot (R-Utah) and Rep. Willis Hawley (R-Oreg.) who sponsored the bill. Some extreme claims have been made about this piece of legislation. Pete du Pont, former Governor of Delaware and aspirant for the presidential nomination, has alleged that Smoot-Hawley not only caused the Great Depression but also led to the rise of Adolf Hitler.[5]

The record debunks such claims. There are two general explanations for the Great Depression. The monetarists blame the depression on the collapse of the banking system, a crisis triggered by bad loans to farmers and the stock market. The wide-spread bank failures led to a drop in the personal money supply, since the loss of deposits and savings was at a time when there was no insurance. The Keynesians blame a general drop in aggregate demand that led to a contraction in output and employment by the business sector. Neither school considers international trade to have played any significant role in the crisis.

Indeed, the father of the Keynesian school, John Maynard Keynes, writing in 1931 after the depression was underway, argued that adding a new tariff would help England work its way out of the downturn. His description of the standard stimulative policy sounds much like a description of the policies followed by the Reagan administration:

... the direct effects of an expansionist policy must be to cause Government borrowing, to throw some burden on the Budget, and to increase our excess of imports. In every way therefore — the opponents of such a policy point out — it will aggravate the want of confidence, the burden of taxation and the international instability, which they believe, are at the bottom of our present troubles.[6]

The question for policymakers is how to get the most out of an expansionist program while minimizing the adverse side-effects. Keynes went on to argue that "there is no possible means of curing unemployment except by restoring to employers a proper margin of profit." He also argued that "the lack of profits in home business inclines the investor to place his money abroad, while high taxation exercises a sinister influence in the same direction," thus also undermining domestic production and employment. He rejected the idea of cutting wages to make British exports cheaper because low wages are not good for either workers or the domestic economy. Low wages will cut domestic demand more than they will expand exports. The need is to boost domestic demand without the government taking on large debts or without the stimulative effect leaking out of the economy and being wasted on imports. Keynes concluded:

> What measures are available to neutralise these dangers? A decision to reform the grave abuses of the dole, and a decision to postpone for the present all new charges on the Budget for social services in order to conserve its resources to meet schemes for the expansion of employment, are advisable and should be taken. *But the main decision which seems to me to-day to be absolutely forced on any wise Chancellor of the Exchequer, whatever his beliefs about Protection, is the introduction of a substantial revenue tariff* [emphasis added].[7]

The solution, in short, is to curtail welfare spending, concentrate on creating jobs and boosting profits, and enact a tariff in place of higher domestic taxes — a sound policy for any era. The tariff would not only bring money into the treasury, but "In so far as it leads to the substitution of home-produced goods for goods previously imported, it will increase employment in the country," since it would also provide some protection to home-based industry. Keynes, one of the most influential economic thinkers of the century, considered tariffs to be part of the solution, not part of the problem, during the Depression.

There was nothing in Smoot-Hawley, or in American tariff history, to contradict this thinking. It is claimed that Smoot-Hawley raised tariffs to record highs and thus collapsed world trade, bringing on the Depression. A look at the calendar will disprove this chain of thought since the bill was passed in 1930 and did not go into effect until 1931. But the stock market crash had already occurred back in 1929. Smoot-Hawley was a response to the downturn, not its precursor.

World trade did collapse during the Depression but, again, this was a result of the downturn, not its cause. With mass unemployment, few people could afford to buy imports or much of anything else. Still, during the Depression, the United States continued to run trade surpluses each year, which was a plus to the economy.

Smoot-Hawley made very minor adjustments in U.S. tariff rates and most of the changes were in agricultural rates. That is why historian Frank Taussig concluded at the time that Smoot-Hawley was enacted that the tariff was "futile . . . . On the important branches of these industries the protective system has already been carried so far that no considerable further displacement of imports could be expected."[8] The United States had had a protective tariff system in place since the turn of the century. Overall rates under protection were less than under the revenue tariff system that had been in effect during most of the 19th century. The protective rates were targeted on specific products whereas revenue rates were levied across the board on all imports.

There had been a sizeable increase in tariff rates under the 1922 Ford-McCumber Act. Duties on covered imports ran on average from 36 percent to 40 percent of value during the 1920s. But rather than trigger a depression, passage of Ford-McCumber was followed by a boom. Real per capita GNP growth from 1923 to 1929 was 3.3 percent per year compared to 2.3 percent for the recent 1982-1987 period.

There is simply no merit, in fact or theory, to the argument that tariffs in general or the Smoot-Hawley tariff in particular have caused depressions in general or the Great Depression in particular. That the advocates of "free trade" have had to resort to such an obviously false analogy in order to make an argument against adopting a trade and industrial policy for the United States is itself a strong indication of the bankruptcy of their own ideas.

The Japanese Trade Situation

Japan has conducted the most significant, wide-scale trade offensive against the United States. As of 1987, the trade deficit with Japan represented 36 percent of the overall U.S. trade imbalance. Dr. Ronald A. Morse of the Library of Congress has written:

> Japan is arguably the most significant country in the world for the United States. If any country surpassed the United States as the world's leading economic power, it will be Japan, not the Soviet Union.[9]

The United States is a weakened superpower today because of Japan's mercantilist assault on its economy. America's freedom of action has been limited by Japan's economic power. Japan already has achieved with the weapons of trade and finance much of what it could not achieve with the weapons of war in the 1930s and 1940s.

An "International" not "Global" Economy

Any economic program for America has to be based on a clear-sighted, comprehensive understanding of Japan's economic objectives, just as any American military defense program has to be based on the objective of the Soviet Union. Central to such an understanding is the fact that the economic struggle of our time is between nations, not simply between companies.

In recent years, Americans have been told that they live in an "information age" in which there is a "global economy." According to George Gilder, who embraces this vision of an economic utopia, "There is no more reason for a balance of trade between the U.S. and Japan than between New York and Ohio."[10] Gilder is consistent in his vision, favoring the repeal of all security restrictions on the sale of high-technology to the Soviet Union and the end of curbs on immigration into the United States. To Gilder, national borders have no meaning. Everything the world over should be free and open, starting with America. In short, Gilder embraces an anti-national one-worldism.

This vision continues to fly in the face of reality. The world just doesn't work this way. West Germany is not California; Japan is not Ohio. American states are not just integrated economically, but politically and culturally as well. This is what makes the states united. Activity within a nation is fundamentally different than activity between nations. So fundamental is this difference that anyone who cannot see it (or will not see it) has so blinded themselves to reality as to render their theories and policy recommendations worthless.

Ohio does not have its own foreign policy or national objectives distinct from that of California or Texas or New York. If a factory moves from Illinois to Georgia, it is far easier for its employees to move with it than if the factory moves from Illinois to Malaysia. Also, the movement of a factory from Illinois to Georgia does not reduce the production capacity or the total jobs available to the United States as a whole, whereas a movement of a factory across the national border does lead to such a reduction in the U.S. economy. The world is still organized on the basis of nation-states, nation-states with historical memories, cultural identities and particular interests. Thus the world has an international economy, not a global economy. Any economic theory, no matter how interestingly crafted within itself, will fail if it attempts to assume away the real world or run against it.

It is a mistake to believe that, just because modern technology has improved communications and transportation between distant spots on the globe, there is not a global system. It takes far more than this to constitute a system. Economics alone cannot do it. The world is actually becoming more dis-integrated. Since the world wars, the number of independent political entities, nation-states, has quadrupled. Religious and ideological antagonisms have multiplied. Though there has been no third world war, there has been a constant din of local and regional wars and revolutions. Violence and instability are on the increase, undermining the confidence needed to erect long-term economic networks or a secure global division of labor. There is no

Pax Romana to provide the essential foundation for a global economy and the United States has neither the will nor the ability to impose or sustain a *Pax Americana.* The country has its hands full just managing its own affairs.

Japan's National Goals

The electronic integration of financial markets is not an unmixed blessing. Christopher Wood notes that "this creates perfect conditions for a chain reaction."[11] The chain reaction can be a global panic. Therefore, American lawmakers and policymakers should be wary of the new globalism. As Ronald Morse stated, "History suggests that the optimistic American view of mutually beneficial independence may be unrealistic." Dr. Morse notes, for instance, that the Japanese "have been ruthless in their penetration of their biggest benefactor's market." They are engaged in what has been described as "adversarial trade," which is the opposite of the kind of complimentary trade envisioned by economic idealists.[12] Whereas West Germany has been more sensitive to American reactions and has been careful to send only 10 percent of its products to the United States, Japan has poured 38 percent of its products into the United States. In dollar terms, the Japanese trade surplus with America is more than three times that of West Germany — $52 billion for Japan in 1986, compared to $15.6 billion for West Germany.

The Japanese still have much to gain from the United States in strategic terms. They want to retain the protective American nuclear umbrella and conventional military shield, especially since this saves them about $50 billion annually they otherwise would have to spend on defense. As Dr. Morse has said, they want to keep this defense shield "at least until Japan emerges as number one." It is clear that the Japanese look to a considerably weaker America by the end of the century. They also clearly hope that they can continue to add strength to their own economy by subtracting strength from the U.S. economy.

With its unique consensus society, involving a high degree of social discipline, cultural harmony and national determination, Japan is well-positioned to attain the pre-eminence that it seeks. With growing Japanese economic power undoubtedly will come political and military power. Ambition is hardly ever confined to one dimension. Far from organizing its efforts on the basis of George Gilder's antinational, globalist model, Japan is moving in the direction of a more intense nationalism. Dr. Morse asserts that "National pride — combined with anti-Americanism, is on the rise" in Japan.

No American wants to seek conflict with Japan, but Americans must come to understand the internal dynamics of the Japanese nation-state. Unfortunately, America's leaders have not understood that the challenge posed by Japan is a profoundly nationalistic one that goes far beyond mere trade surpluses. It is on Japan's overall national objectives that Congress and the next Administration must concentrate, not simply on imports and exports.

Country-Specific Retaliation

An examination of the role of Japan, South Korea, West Germany, Brazil and the People's Republic of China as well as certain other nations underscores the need to deal with trade problems on a country-specific basis.

Robert T. Green and Trina L. Larsen of the University of Texas at Austin have outlined a strategy of selective retaliation against U.S. trade adversaries. They reject the idea of imposing tariffs on all U.S. trading partners. Instead, they urge retaliatory policies that are "country specific" and that "focus only on nations whose practices hurt U.S. trade." Green and Larsen point out that "Japan accounts for more than one quarter" of the U.S. trade deficit, adding that "another handful of nations — Brazil, South Korea, Taiwan, West Germany and Hong Kong" account for an additional quarter of the deficit.[13]

"To hit the deficit where it hurts us most, we need a target rifle, not a shotgun," conclude Green and Larsen. Under their plan, sustained bilateral trade deficits would trigger automatic U.S. quotas. If the trade deficit with a particular country were to rise above a set level, a requirement to reduce the deficit by a certain percentage would automatically go into effect. The country affected would then be forced to do one of three things: "open more of its market to U.S. products, restrict certain exports to the United States, [or] institute an across the board quota on all products to the United States."

This proposal for country specific retaliation offers a perfectly reasonable way for dealing with foreign targeting, dumping, export subsidization or other unfair trade practices and strategies intended to damage the American economy. With such a system as law, America's trade competitors undoubtedly would find it prudent to enter into bilateral negotiations with Washington that would eliminate problems before retaliation was triggered.

Of course, no single measure will solve all of America's trade problems. There may be cases where the United States will need to run trade deficits with particular countries in order to acquire sufficient quantities of critical raw materials, fuels or other inputs not generally available elsewhere. This will require that the United States run trade surpluses elsewhere to compensate. And, there will be cases where certain strategic industries will need to be protected against rival imports, even from countries with which the United States has balanced trade or a surplus. But these situations, like country specific retaliation itself, point up that economic problems need to be handled case by case, on terms best suited to advance American interests.

Dollar Devaluation

At the Bonn economic summit of 1985, President Reagan urged a multilateral effort to drive down the value of the dollar. The dollar has been in sharp decline ever since. By mid-1988, the dollar had lost 50 percent of its value measured against a trade-weighted marketbasket of other currencies. In the process it set a series of post-World War II record lows against the Japanese yen. No action of any significance was taken to deal with the flood of imports directly. Indeed, the Reagan Administration bitterly opposed trade measures with any teeth in them, clinging to out-moded slogans about "free trade" while watching whole industries being devastated.

While the administration engaged in currency devaluation, it never used the term "devaluation" in public and carefully sought to hide from the American people the full meaning of its policy. The dollar was talked down in a very clever way. In most countries, currency devaluation results in political upheaval and has often forced governments to resign. Devaluation means that the purchasing power of the dollar is falling in world markets. Another word for this, which again the administration never used, is inflation.

The policy of talking down the dollar aroused little opposition when it was announced, because it was billed as an active policy to deal with the trade deficit. In reality, it was not an active policy. It was a decision to do nothing and let the market take its course. Given the size of the trade deficit and the large balance of payments deficit it produced, a decline in the dollar was inevitable. The Reagan Administration has attempted to give the impression that it is in control of events and that everything that is happening is part of a carefully-thought policy. In reality, both the flood of imports and the collapse of the dollar have been completely out of control, but administration officials have not dared to admit it.

William Niskanen, who served on the Council of Economic Advisers from 1981 to 1985, has admitted that the trade deficit caught the administration by surprise. Scant attention was paid to the effect of domestic policy on the trade situation, and the concept of a growing trade war was apparently never examined at all. After a century of being a surplus/creditor nation, no one foresaw the sudden change in America's fortune. Once the crisis was upon the country, the administration was paralyzed by a mixture of ideological rigidity and political expediency. It opted for trying to explain away the problem rather than acting to solve it.[14]

The inadequacy of a policy to balance trade purely by expanding exports has already been examined. Foreign industrial policies and Third World debt keep overseas markets limited. There is no guarantee that higher aggregate exports will save the particular strategic industries America needs. Selling more timber and oranges will not help strengthen the U.S. computer and steel industries. However, another dimension of devaluation needs to be mentioned. The Claremont Economics Institute points out that a drop in the value of the dollar would do "absolutely nothing to help most American producers."[15] This has proven correct. The additional goods American companies are exporting are being sold at half price. The terms of trade are moving against the United States. Foreigners are now receiving more real goods and services in exchange for what they send us. And, as long as foreigners are able to continue earning money from a trade surplus with America, they can continue to buy American assets at bargain prices.

Devaluation, however, does not just make U.S. goods cheaper. It also makes foreign goods more expensive. That is why devaluation is a form of inflation. The Reagan Administration has been quiet about this because it contradicts its overall attitude towards imports. If countries do not act to restrict imports, the market will do it for them through devaluation. As imports become more expensive, people will buy fewer of them. In the simple market model, a 50 percent devaluation is no different than a 100 percent across-the-board tariff. The effect of both is to double the price of foreign goods. However, given the adamant stand of the administration against tariffs or other import restrictions, it cannot admit that the effect of its devaluation policy is the same as tariffs. Such an admission would raise the question as to why the administration is so opposed to one policy as a matter of principle, and so eager to pursue the other.

This preference is not confined to government officials. Robert Eisner, an economics professor at Northwestern University and president of the American Economics Association, has stated that "it is vital that the dollar be allowed to drop as far as market conditions dictate if we are to protect and advance American jobs without protectionism."[16] But why choose devaluation over protectionism if both will accomplish the same ends? It doesn't make much sense except in terms of abstract philosophy. Dollar devaluation can be said to be the result of the invisible hand of the market and thus be acceptable within a free trade policy, even when abetted by central bankers. Direct policy measures, of course, represent a visible hand and are unacceptable to free traders.

Yet, traditionally, given a choice between devaluation and tariffs or import quotas to eliminate a trade deficit, most economists and statesmen have favored a direct policy of restricting selected imports rather than an indirect monetary policy that affects all imports. This is because the United States does need to import some products which it cannot obtain domestically and/or which are vital inputs for the production of other goods. Dollar devaluation makes these needed imports more expensive when it is in the national interest for them to be cheap. There are other imports, chiefly consumer goods, that have no particular strategic merit and could be imported without problem. But, the prices of these goods are also increased by devaluation.

Meanwhile, strategic heavy and high-tech industries under attack by rival industrial powers need to be protected. They do receive some aid from the increase in import prices that result from devaluation, but not as much as if a policy was enacted with their needs specifically in mind. Devaluation, by spreading its effect across the entire economy, applies pressure where none is needed or where it is harmful, and it fails to apply enough pressure where it is truly needed. This shotgun approach more often hits the wrong target than the right one. It does more damage to general trade than the targeted policy of specific restriction.

This simple model is complicated by the fact that many commodities on the world market are priced in terms of dollars even when they do not originate in the United States. As the dollar drops in value, these commodities become cheaper to most countries (whose purchasing power is increasing) but not to America. Oil is an example. Its price is always quoted in dollars. The Japanese and the Europeans have seen the price of oil, in terms of their currencies, drop by 50 percent more than has the United States. This means that the cost of production in Europe and Japan is lower relative to production in the United States by the amount of this difference in effective oil prices. Wolfgang F. Stopler, Emeritus Professor of Economics at the University of Michigan, warned of this effect:

> It should be realized that the decline in the dollar price of oil is just as great for Japan and West Germany as it is for us, and that the yen and Deutsche mark price of their oil imports is falling even more by the lower value of the dollar in terms of yens and marks. Thus their economies will be stimulated even more ... their economies will increase in competitiveness with ours.[17]

By the same token, when the value of the dollar is high, the effective price of oil is pushed up for Japan and the Europeans, but not for Americans. This gives an edge to the United States.

Devaluation is considered a sign of economic weakness which the manipulation of currency values can only disguise, but not correct. This is because the value of a currency reflects the health of the economy and its competitiveness in comparison with rivals. When a currency rises in value, it is a sign that the economy is "winning"; when it falls, it is a sign that the economy is "losing." The international currency exchange is like a giant stock market, with each dollar, yen, mark, franc, and pound acting like a share of national stock. The strength of a currency is more than just an indicator, however; it is also an asset.

Money and Power

During most of the post-war period, the United States was able to run trade surpluses even as it ran balance-of-payments deficits. The balance-of-payments deficit was the result of two factors related to America's role as a superpower. First were the foreign outlays associated with the projection of American power: the deployment of military units overseas and the outlays for foreign aid. Second were the outflows of capital for foreign investment. This caused a considerable amount of concern among critics of American "imperialism" who saw it as an attempt to control production worldwide; it also gladdened the hearts of proponents of American power. Of course, foreign investment is meant to earn a profit, and when that profit is repatriated to the United States it is a plus to the balance of payments. For some three decades, the surpluses earned from the favorable trade balance and from foreign investment income provided most of the funds needed to support the global projection of American power and the expansion of American business overseas.

That the surpluses were not high enough to cover the entire outflow was a constant threat to the strength of the dollar. When the negative balance grew during the Vietnam War, the dollar had to be devalued, in 1971. The last link to gold was severed and the Bretton Woods system collapsed. A return to fixed exchange rates and a gold standard is impossible as long as the United States continues to run large balance of payments deficits.

Today, the problem is worse than in 1971. At its core is the massive U.S. trade deficit. In 1971, the trade deficit was only $2.9 billion.

Today, it will be considered a great improvement if it drops to $130 billion in 1988. The trade deficit swamps everything else in the international economic equation. As long as the deficit continues, so will the downward pressure on the dollar, with continued negative consequences for American power. The trade deficit has converted the United States into a net debtor; foreigners earn more in income from investments in the United States than Americans earn from their investments elsewhere. This flow of investment funds is the only positive element in the U.S. balance of payments equation. However, to insure that this flow continues will require that American maintain high real interest rates, which is bad for the domestic economy.

In 1985, Daniel Burstein warned that "The dollar cost of buying land and opening factories in America is a bargain for Japanese companies operating from a yen-based economy." In some industries, Burstein said, "American workers are now considered cheap labor."[18] Unfortunately, the nation's political leaders did not understand that a low dollar policy in a period of continued trade deficits and an "open economy" would push the United States in the direction of a less-developed country.

Not all nations want market adjustment. Deficit states want to get rid of their deficits, but surplus states want to continue their surpluses. As C. Fred Bergsten has observed:

> ... mercantilist countries fiercely resist taking any adjustment initiatives when in surplus. They generally prefer to finance deficit countries, even when weighed against adjustment initiatives of the latter. Their mercantilist desire for ample liquidity for themselves generally leads them to support large-scale creation of global liquidity, as Japan has done.[19]

And why not? Moving the financial capital of the world from New York to Tokyo, as it once moved from London to New York, will expand Japan's control over economic activity, both now and in the future. West Germany also falls in this mercantilist category.

Mercantilist states want to continue the benefits of high production, employment and capital creation gained by surpluses. In addition to resisting currency adjustments, they may simply lower their profit margins in the short run in order to maintain market share. The price of their imports will then rise less than the amount of the devaluation. This is a form of investment in the future. It is well known that Japanese firms will operate at a loss in foreign markets rather than cut back production or lay off workers. It is not just a matter of receiving subsidies from Tokyo that leads them to stay in business under conditions that would force American firms to fold. The idea is that surviving in the short run will lead to larger markets and profits in the long-run. Once foreign industries come to dominate the market, higher prices will simply work to their advantage.

The fall in the value of the dollar also marks a fall in the American standard of living. This is not the message from those who insist that America is in a period of unparalleled expansion. However, other economic experts have clearly expressed a less pleasant interpretation. One of these experts is Alfred L. Malabre, Jr., news editor of *The Wall Street Journal*. Regarding "the dollar-dominated decline," Mr. Malabre said:

> Most Americans have begun to endure a drop in their living standards, and with so little protest that little attention has yet to be paid to such a striking development, such an important economic and political event.[20]

Devaluation is an attempt to deal with the trade deficit using a policy of austerity and retrenchment rather than domestic expansion and import-substitution. This road leads to a recession, the usual "market" correction for persistent trade deficits. Some businessmen and economists like the policy of devaluation, but that is because they see only the short-term jump in U.S. exports. The results, however, are short-term also and purchased at a very high price. Given the side effects of devaluation, it is a far more radical "solution" to the trade deficit than are targeted import restrictions. Under the Reagan Administration's policy, the priorities were backwards. Rather than gut the dollar to balance trade, the United States should be trying to balance trade in order to maintain the value of the dollar.

Chapter VI

The Political Economy of National Power

> In modern times — with the rise of the national state, the expansion of European civilization throughout the world, the industrial revolution and the steady advance of military technology — we have constantly been confronted with the interrelationship of commercial, financial, and industrial strength on the one hand, and political and military strength on the other. This interrelationship is one of the most critical and absorbing problems of statesmanship.
>
> Edward Mead Earle
> *Makers of Modern Strategy*, 1941

The Military-Industrial Base

Part of the longevity of Edward Mead Earle's classic essay is due to the fact that, despite the rapid growth of strategic thinking and writing after World War II, economic planning has usually been a missing component in national security policy formulation. Compared to other areas of research on matters of defense and foreign policy, few authors have carried on Earle's work. In the United States, the interrelationship between economic and military strength has unfortunately not been one of "the most critical and absorbing problems of statesmanship."

Why? Economic policy has been considered to be part of domestic rather than foreign policy. Except for agriculture, international trade has historically played a small role in the economy. Until recently, events overseas have had little effect on employment and prices in the

United States. Furthermore, economics is the preserve of the private sector; national security is the responsibility of the state. Though government intervention in the economy has grown steadily since the New Deal, its character has been determined by the interplay of domestic interest groups competing for the power to redistribute wealth internally. This has undermined the ability to craft economic policy in the interests of the nation as a whole.

It was not always this way. The Founding Fathers showed a profound appreciation for the economic foundations of national greatness. They were quite aware of the world of power politics that formed the background to their bid for an independent United States that would expand across the continent. The nation's first Secretary of the Treasury, Alexander Hamilton, penned the classic American statement of economic strategy in his 1791 *Report on Manufactures*, which aimed to promote a diversified, industrial economy that would "tend to render the United States independent of foreign nations for military and other essential supplies." He advocated a wide range of policies, including subsidies and tariffs, to promote American industry.

Even Hamilton's arch-rival, Thomas Jefferson, was shocked into rethinking his anti-industrial/free-trade posture, because of the War of 1812. Writing to the French classical economist Jean Baptiste Say, Jefferson cited experience as the best source to answer the question of whether "profit or preservation is the first interest of the State." He thought that history favored the latter:

> The prohibiting duties we lay on all articles of foreign manufacture which prudence requires us to establish at home, with the patriotic determination of every good citizen to use no foreign articles which can be made within ourselves, without regard to difference of price, secures us against a relapse into foreign dependency.[1]

War has often shattered the rose-colored glasses that distort the vision of politicians, philosophers and the people. The world wars and the global instability in the years since 1945 have clearly demonstrated the need to maintain a large industrial base for mobilization in case of war, crisis or a disruption of trade. As the House

Armed Services Committee stated in 1980, "It is a contradiction to think that we can maintain our position as a first-class military power with a second-class industrial base."[2]

Adam Smith, in his seminal work, *The Wealth of Nations*, established that the source of a nation's wealth is its capacity to produce. Though free traders trace their doctrine back to Smith, he himself was aware that the capacity to produce was also the source of power for nations. Here, he was in agreement with the mercantilists. He even made an exception to his general free trade theory, saying "defense is more important than opulence" and endorsing the Navigation Acts. These famous Acts gave British ships a monopoly of the carrying trade of the Empire. Military historian Corelli Barnett has argued that the number of industries needing this kind of protection has increased since Smith wrote:

> Adam Smith erected "scientific theory" out of the passing circumstances of his own era. He could not foresee that national defense would come to depend not just on seaman and naval stores, but on total industrial and economic capability. He could not foresee the effects of the most revolutionary technological developments in the history of mankind.[3]

Adam Smith overlooked the main development: "wars of production" would dominate future battlefields and arms races. Unlike agriculture or mining, where endowments of soil, climate and mineral deposits produce a division of labor that could be called natural, manufacturing establishments could be built almost anywhere. In the real world, the classic concept of comparative advantage no longer held. The balance of industrial power can be changed, whether by the private actions of multinational corporations or by the industrial policies of ambitious governments.

Economic Mobilization

In a crisis, the industrial sector will have to be mobilized to meet national needs. This means that the definition of strategic industry must be broadened beyond just the peacetime defense establishment.

The now-defunct Joint Congressional Committee on Defense Production argued in 1977 that the defense industrial base:

> comprises not only those industries which are considered primarily or potentially military in nature, but also processing, refining and other basic industries; the manufacturers and suppliers of components, subassemblies, and spare parts; research and development laboratories; industrial plant equipment which is or could be available for defense production; and the management resources and skilled labor pool required to operate these facilities.[4]

Secretary of Defense Caspar Weinberger warned in his 1985 Report to Congress that:

> While the U.S. industrial base was experiencing its greatest decline in history, with detrimental effects on both civilian and defense sectors, the Soviet Union was rapidly expanding its industrial base, which is overwhelmingly dedicated to armaments production.[5]

Many strategic industries are under siege by imports. By 1986, foreign producers had captured 26 percent of the U.S. market for steel, 37 percent for machine tools, 60 percent of consumer electronics, over 27 percent for automobiles, 34 percent of wide-bodied jet aircraft and over 60 percent for industrial robots. The ferroalloy industry is near collapse. Mineral refining is moving offshore. Shipbuilding is kept afloat only by government contracts. Sectors threatened run the spectrum from the older "smoke stack" industries to the newest "high-tech" fields. The struggle for control of world industry will be fought for the rest of this century. The winners will be able to influence not only the world's economy, but the world's politics as well.[6]

1988 Trade Balances in Selected Strategic Industries[7]
(in $ billions, + surplus, − deficit)

Aerospace	+13.2
Chemicals	+10.0
Computer Equipment	+ 2.8
Electronics	− 2.0
Machine Tools	− 1.1
Steel	−18.7
Vehicles	−45.0

Robert C. Fabrie, a Senior Fellow at the Mobilization Concepts Development Center of National Defense University, has argued that:

> the fact that needed manufactured products could be made off-shore more cheaply ... does not offer a viable alternative if we look at the potential reliability of these suppliers with cold logic. How secure would the nation be at the outbreak of a war if 50 or 60 percent of the goods, technology, production processes or equipment needed by this nation for mobilization had to be obtained quickly from a foreign source?[8]

An alarmist prediction? Or is the danger already upon us? Admiral Carlisle A. H. Trost, Chief of Naval Operations, had this to say in his testimony to the Armed Service Committee in February 1987: "If foreign sources were cut off, M-1 tank production would stop, critical subsystems for the F-16 fighter would be delayed, and semiconductors for a host of aerospace programs would be unavailable."[9] This points up the fact that, according to the State Department, as much as 88 percent of all U.S. manufacturing uses some foreign-produced components.[10] Even apparently strong sectors of industry may be vulnerable to foreign disruption.

From steel to computer chips, machine tools to shipbuilding, the American economy is not keeping up with the nation's strategic needs. As the gap between needs and capabilities widens and is filled with imports, the vulnerability of the nation increases and its power diminishes. Strategic economist William P. Wadbrook, while serving as head of the Federal Emergency Management Agency, noted that:

> Our allies and trade partners, noncontiguous, non-subjected, and with interests intermingled with those of the great international firms, affect strategic imports (including energy), D-day support requirements, and today even weapons system production ... the obvious strategy for an adversary is to nibble at our worldwide resource tentacles and watch the fun. It need hardly be asked whether this scenario is not already in progress.[11]

Needed is a policy to selectively protect heavy and high-technology industries and their supporting infrastructure. The obvious candidate industries are steel, autos, chemicals, machine tools, computers, electronics, telecommunications, metal processing, heavy equipment, energy, aerospace and shipbuilding.

More than just money and jobs are at stake. Military power depends on industrial capacity and technological innovation. Stephen S. Cohen and John Zysman, economists from the University of California at Berkeley, have argued:

> An erosion of our competitive position in a critical set of industrial chains would constitute a massive reduction in our strategic independence and diplomatic options. Diverse, robust and leading-edge U.S. producers in [semiconductors, computers, telecommunications, robotics, machine tools] and other industrial chains are more critical to U.S. national security at the current time than to most other nations ... whatever the ups and downs of military spending, our basic security posture is built on the assumption that America will maintain, round after hurried round, a permanent lead in a rather broad range of advanced industrial technologies.[12]

The economies of scale in manufacturing and the high cost of research and development make a large commercial industrial sector a necessity. Industry lowers the cost of producing military equipment because much of the fixed cost of production and research are carried by the commercial side of the enterprise. In peacetime, private American firms must be able to maintain the productive capacity and research and development programs needed for an emergency. Otherwise, either the government will have to maintain its own reserve capacity at enormous public expense or the nation will have to be dependent on uncertain foreign supplies. Both are high-risk, high-cost alternatives to the protection and support of a large and on-going commercial industrial base.

Trade with the Soviets

Since the earliest years of the Soviet regime, a number of leading American companies have imagined that it is possible to carry on lucrative trade with the USSR and to build plants in its territory.

Tractors, trucks and other types of American-designed machinery were manufactured in the Soviet Union within a few years of the Bolshevik Revolution. Occidental Petroleum chairman Armand Hammer, Lenin's first American friend, has promoted business ventures with the Soviets since the 1920s. And, he has intertwined his role as entrepreneur with that of apologist for every regime from Lenin and Stalin to Brezhnev and Gorbachev.

During World War II, the United States furnished the USSR not only with military equipment and munitions but also with technology and industrial materials to aid the expansion of Soviet factories. This did not win the lasting friendship of Moscow, which initiated the Cold War even before 1945. During the detente of the Nixon years, the United States again pursued a policy that sought to improve relations through increased transfers of American technology and equipment to the USSR, including the construction of "turn-key" manufacturing plants. Again, this effort failed. These transfers did not lead to international goodwill. They merely increased Moscow's ability to carry out its aggressive designs, which included the largest peacetime military buildup in history.

Trucks produced in American-built Soviet factories were used to carry North Vietnamese troops across Southeast Asia, Cuban troops across Africa and Soviet troops across Afghanistan. Precision ball bearings produced by American-designed machines were used to improve the accuracy of Soviet ICBMs aimed at America. While the American people and Congress were deeply offended by the Soviet Union's violations of human rights and escalation of the arms race, those who sought to gain personal profits from doing business with the totalitarian regime never faltered in their efforts to expand trade.

In the mid-1970s, the US-USSR Trade and Economic Council (USTEC) was established, with a joint board consisting of American corporate representatives and senior officials of Soviet economic agencies, including the so-called US-USSR Chamber of Commerce. A Lieutenant General of the KGB has been assigned to the US-USSR Chamber of Commerce board of directors. Though highly secretive in its operations, USTEC has continually pressed for new trade links with Moscow and an end to restrictions on the transfer of strategic technology. USTEC argues that economics is a matter of private business concern that should be kept separate from issues involving Soviet repression or aggression. Here again, the naive and dangerous sophistry that global economics and international power politics have nothing to do with each other raises its head.

In 1987, the long-time head of USTEC, C. William Verity, Jr., was named Secretary of Commerce by President Reagan. Verity immediately began a major push to open new avenues of trade with the USSR. Large delegations of corporate executives from major U.S. companies were sent to Moscow, though the Commerce Department consistently refused to disclose the names of those who participated in these meetings with senior Soviet officials. The climate of euphoria created in the United States by Mikhail Gorbachev's policies of *glasnost* and *perestroika* have greatly facilitated Verity's efforts. Though Gorbachev's reform movement has been more talk than action, it has created an environment that can best be described as Detente II.

The appointment of Verity, and President Reagan's apparent conversion to the old formula of economic "bridge-building" between East and West, marks a radical change from the administration's policies during its early years in office. When President Reagan first took office, he initiated a series of negotiations with America's allies to tighten up restrictions on trade with the Soviet bloc. By 1984 new controls were in place for computers and computer chips, electronics and communications equipment, robotics, aerospace and high-tech manufacturing technologies. In February 1987, however, Reagan initiated another review of policy, this time aimed at loosening restrictions.

Detente is not the only motive behind this reversal. The administration is determined to solve the trade deficit by boosting exports rather than by curtailing imports. However, as already argued, foreign export markets are limited. This has led the administration ot the desperate act of looking at the Soviet bloc as a way out of the trade deficit — another example of short-term thinking undermining the long-term security of the country.

This policy is more foolish because it will fail to accomplish even its short-term objective. The Kremlin's rulers have no desire to expend their limited foreign exchange on mass-consumption items.

The Soviets want to buy capital equipment to construct their own production facilities. They won't allow the United States to create the kind of large export market of finished products that it needs to balance its huge inflow of imports.

It is easy to understand the USSR's desire to acquire advanced technology and production methods from the West, especially when the West is willing to provide the equipment and willing to pay for it with credit financing on easy terms. It is a major strategic mistake to confuse Gorbachev's desire to restructure and modernize the Soviet economy with a desire to convert the USSR into a peace-loving democracy. Realism would argue just the opposite. Gorbachev's reforms seek to develop the Soviet military-industrial-technological base by altering work habits and morale, improving incentives and efficiency, and utilizing Western capital and technology.

Popular opinion in the West equates economic reform with social progress, but this is unwarranted optimism. The Communist Party will still decide the allocation of resources in the USSR and nothing so far suggests that the Red Army will lose its top priority ranking in the economy. Soviet weapons production has not been slowed by Gorbachev. The USSR continues to outproduce the United States in most categories of military equipment, even with the modest Reagan rearmament effort.

Does the United States really want its most dangerous enemy to improve its economic base? A careful examination of Russian history reveals the error in the thinking of advocates of economic detente. Peter the Great, the founder of modern Russia, set the precedent now followed by Gorbachev. The farseeing 18th century czar modernized Russia by altering customs and introducing methods imported from Western Europe. By combining modern equipment with Russia's large population and resources, under autocratic direction, Peter and his imperial successors created a new Great Power that in time expanded across Central Asia and the Far East to become, in territory, the world's largest empire-state. The Soviets gave to this empire renewed energy and ideological drive after the revolution, leading it to further expansion, the domination of Eastern Europe and Superpower status. Moscow has repeatedly turned to the West during this period for fresh infusions of the means to support its ambitions.

Writing in the Spring 1988 issue of *Orbis*, the journal of the Foreign Policy Research Institute, Professor Aron Katsenelinboigen, a Russian expatriate teaching at the University of Pennsylvania's Wharton School, argues that Gorbachev's policies are compatible with a return to a virulent nationalism.[13] This is the same drive that motivated the Russophile reform movement of 150 years ago. It has never been completely abandoned. That movement started out with a liberal agenda but found that liberalism was too weak a doctrine. It then turned to an anti-liberal chauvinism and the belief that Russia was destined to dominate the world because its culture was superior to the decadent individualism of the West.

Soviet leaders have returned to the nationalist theme when the system was in trouble. Lenin proclaimed the New Economic Policy in the 1920s. Stalin rallied the population to the defense of Mother Russia, not the Bolshevik Revolution, during World War II. Today, according to Prof. Katsenelinboigen, nationalism is growing among intellectuals, particularly historians. Groups like Otechestvo (Fatherland) and Pamyat (Memory) have a wide following. One anonymous dissident is quoted as saying, "The era of Westernizing and democracy or the aspirations for these has disappeared . . . now the dominant trend is Russian patriotism and ethnic awareness." Lev Timofeyev, an economist and journalist, has warned that the future could bring "a military dictatorship with strong xenophobic overtones, a hybrid between Pinochet and the Ayatollah."

In line with this danger is the rise of paramilitary street gangs that follow a puritanical regime of physical fitness and martial arts. They see themselves as reformers out to rejuvenate Soviet society. They attack people who attend rock concerts or who drink alcohol in public. And they denounce corruption in high places as treason. Such gangs exist in many major cities including Moscow and Leningrad. Katsenelinboigen believes that the KGB and the Komsomol covertly support these gangs. The gangs "are solving a problem the army has failed to address: how a cynical society could produce tough, ruthless soldiers . . . . Their potential military value keeps these gangs from being stamped out."[14]

There is great danger in any U.S. policy that weakens opposition to strategic trade with the Soviets or permits the transfer of technology needed by Moscow. It is extremely foolish to provide the USSR with massive credits that would allow Moscow to build up its power at our expense. The new detentists, both in government and the private sector, fail to see — or greed blinds them to seeing — that aid to the Soviet Union is completely contrary to the national interests of the United States. A "new and improved" Soviet economy would only provide the Kremlin with the means to build more threatening weapons systems and to engage in a more intense political-military struggle around the world. U.S. trade with the Soviet Union should be limited to agricultural commodities and consumer goods which are desired by the Russian people rather than the factories and high-tech equipment desired by the Soviet leaders. In all cases, the USSR should be required to pay for its own purchases.

NSC and CEA Changes

With the new importance of strategic economic policy, it is clear that change is required in the roles and organization of the National Security Council (NSC) and the Council of Economic Advisors (CEA). Congress would do well to broaden the role of the National Security Council and merge the Council of Economic Advisors into it.

Under today's conditions, it is both artificial and harmful to separate strategic economic policy from general national security issues. As the CEA has operated in recent years, it has addressed domestic economic issues in isolation, without due consideration of the effect of policy decisions on overall national strength and the place of the United States in the world. The aims and power of other nations in relation to the American economy has received even less attention. Yet, these factors are crucial to understanding what the United States should do in the economic sphere.

The NSC has been without a mandate to address the impact of broad economic developments on national security. It was established to cut across the administrative borders of myriad government agencies and create a professional staff to coordinate policy and fashion strategy in a comprehensive manner. Trade should be a natural subject for the NSC, but it isn't. International trade is, by definition, part of foreign policy, and foreign policy cannot be rationally considered outside the context of national security. But, science and industry are the foundations of the national economy and military strength. No policy can be considered complete without taking these elements into account. If the NSC is to fulfill its mission and provide the Executive with the best possible basis for decisionmaking, its oversight must include economics.

Chapter VII

The Political Economy of National Wealth

Strategic Industry

The importance of a strong and diversified industrial base is not confined to facilitating military mobilization, as important as that capability is. An industrial base is also essential to the long-term process of economic growth. The British economist A. P. Thirlwill, after a lengthy study of deindustrialization, found eight major advanced capitalist economies — including the United States — that had experienced an absolute decline in manufacturing employment between 1966 and 1981. Thirlwill argued that such declines are necessarily harmful because "manufacturing possesses certain growth-inducing characteristics that other sectors of the economy do not have."[1]

In this sense, a strategic industry is one that is involved either as the prime mover or as a vital supporting sector in the process of economic growth. Economic growth can take two forms: an increase in the output of existing goods and services, or the introduction of new and different goods and services. The first is primarily the result of increased productivity; the second, primarily the result of innovation. Both depend on technology backed by capital accumulation.

Unfortunately, most standard economic models do not adequately deal with the dynamics of change, particularly innovation. They are basically static. A prime example of a static model is the classical theory of comparative advantage upon which free trade theory rests. Under comparative advantage, countries specialize in whatever they do best at a given point in time, letting other areas fade away. There are no strategic industries. Each country relies on imports to provide for its other needs. The efficiency of specialization gives each country an initial increase in economic performance. Each may achieve further growth by improving productivity in the chosen field, but, by specialization, each greatly reduces its chances of achieving the larger, long-term gains from innovation.

Julian Gresser has stated the case:

> [The] static interpretation of comparative advantage produces the following problem. If a country bypasses its growth-inducing strategic industry for the short-term benefits of comparative efficiency, it is possible that that country's long-run productivity would fall, and so also would its standard of living. The country's natural trading partners would grow wealthier by focusing on their strategic sectors.[2]

This is not a new argument, only a neglected one. Friedrich List said essentially the same thing in 1846 when he rejected the notion that vital industries be allowed to collapse because of a momentary change in global prices, asking, "Who would be consoled for the loss of an arm by the knowledge that he could now buy his shirts forty percent cheaper?" This outlook has been enacted into the industrial policies of most advanced nations, particularly Japan and France, where often heard is the slogan, "There are no obsolete industries, only obsolete technologies."

Manufacturing is the central front in this global struggle to capture new technology. This technology, Stephen Cohen and John Zysman argue, is "revolutionizing production . . . creating a fundamental economic transition that puts the position of every nation in the international hierarchy of wealth and power, including the United States, up for grabs."[3]

By value-added, manufacturing directly generates 24 percent of GNP. Cohen and Zysman add to this figure an additional 25 percent of GNP for services "tightly linked" to manufacturing. The linkage makes manufacturing responsible for about half, 49 percent, of GNP.[4] Cohen and Zysman say "industrial chains" link a number of manufacturing and service sectors. Telecommunications is one example among the many they cite: "Will American companies dominate international trade in communications if they are not leaders in computers, semiconductors, telephone switching equipment, launchers, satellites and fiber optics?"[5]

The answer is no, and our rivals understand this. Foreign industrial policies target key links in the chain, hoping that if they can capture a few strategic pieces, the rest of the industrial chain can be pulled under their control. Most high-tech products are producer goods, not consumer goods. Lasers, robots, computers, bioengineering, and machine tools are all linked to improved methods of production. "America must control the production of those high-tech products it invents," write Cohen and Zysman, for two reasons. First, "production is where the lion's share of value-added is realized. It is where the 'rent on innovation' is captured." The profits come from using the technology, not in developing it. Without an industrial base, research and development becomes too expensive to sustain. Second:

> Unless R&D is tightly tied to the manufacturing of the product — to the permanent process of innovation in production now required for competitiveness in manufacturing — R&D will fall behind the cutting edge of incremental innovation.[6]

In short, you cannot control what you cannot produce. Strategic industries are valuable for their own potential, and for their contribution to general scientific advancement, or for their ability to trigger or support developments in other sectors. However, the nature of innovation is unpredictable, non-linear and risky. Public policy must aim at maintaining an industrial base that is broad enough to generate ideas born of synergetic combinations across sectors, and deep enough to provide applications and a market that makes innovation economically viable. The policy tools available are as old as science itself: support for research and education; steps to reduce the financial risk of development; incentives for capital formation and investment; and acquisition and protection of a market base large enough for economies of scale and profitable sales.

Critical Service Industries

While the Legislative and Executive branches address the fiscal and trade deficits and associated problems during the next four years, they cannot afford to neglect the critical service industries. These are the industries upon which much of the future well-being and wealth of the United States will depend.

Among these industries are banking, communications, insurance, medical care, engineering, transportation, construction, merchandising and housing. To suggest that these industries are important does not mean that manufacturing will fade away or become less central to the economy. Many of these services are designed to be complementary to heavy industry and other traditional types of manufacturing. Services will no more replace industry than industry replaced agriculture. Just as the United States remained the leading agricultural country as it became the leading industrial power, it must retain its industrial strength as it expands into services. A healthy economy is a balanced economy.

The American people and their leaders need a better appreciation of competition between nations in the service sectors. These industries make substantial use of computerization and advanced technologies. They manage information essential for the operations of a modern economy. The United States is not lacking in these industries or backward in developing advanced technologies. It is the world leader in many areas. The question is, what needs to be done to make Americans realize that they cannot afford to think that their leadership in critical services will be automatically maintained? Foreign competitors are deeply involved in selling their services to Americans and in acquiring ownership of critical service companies created by Americans. They make extensive use of technology originated in U.S. labs. For instance, Japan as a small group of islands feels the need to disperse its economic activities throughout the globe. As already noted, Japan has moved into banking and finance in a major way. Japanese business interests will undoubtedly move into insurance and other critical service industries in the same way.

The United States, occupying a large and, until recently, secure continental mass, does not feel the same urgency as Japan does. The same can be said of the Canadians. As a result, neither North American country has a strategy for maintaining control of their service sectors during this period of expansion and innovation.

Robert W. Galvin, chairman of Motorola, Inc., the giant American electronics company, has urged a national strategy for the service sector that "will require national dedication." As an entrepreneur, Mr. Galvin wants a strategy that will be built around free enterprise. He wants this strategy to be "shaped primarily by businessmen's guidance" but that must also include federal participation.[7]

To date, little has been done to ensure America's future leadership in the critical service industries. Only one consortium of U.S. computer companies has been created by way of a special dispensation of the federal government. This is minor league strategy next to the efforts mounted by foreign combines. In Japan, MITI drew up a masterplan in 1981 to build a Fifth Generation supercomputer by 1989. This was a joint project of the government and six major private firms: Fujitsu, Hitachi, Toshiba, Oki, NEC and Mitsubishi. New technology developed during the project will belong to the government, which will then share it with all participating private firms on a license basis. MITI has two goals in this operation. First, it wants to develop new technology as rapidly as possible by combining the talents of its most capable corporations. Second, it wants to strengthen all Japanese firms against foreign rivals. Tokyo's philosophy of political economy is not to increase internal competition between Japanese firms, which is the purpose of American antitrust policy for U.S. firms.

The United States has experience with the first part of this kind of strategy. In the NASA space program, it fostered technological development by encouraging corporate cooperation. This strategy needs to be applied to a wider range of projects.

American antitrust law is a serious impediment to the mobilizing of private sector resources and to a successful national strategy to compete in the international economy. This must change. The present complex of laws and regulations must be adjusted to face the challenges posed by foreign combines. The United States cannot afford to lose the struggle over critical service industries. If America loses its leadership in these fields, its wealth and power will be greatly diminished by the early 21st century.

Takeovers and Business Organization

Often overlooked in discussions of economics is the importance of having economic institutions that are compatible with cultural and political traditions. Dr. Charles H. Ferguson has asserted that "economic institutions in the U.S. are no longer functioning as well as they used to function." He said that "What's going on here is the decay of the American industrial system."[8] This decay in the American world of business and industry has nothing to do with the foreign economic challenge, international trade or related factors. Dr. Ferguson pointed to "a massive disinvestment . . . in organizations, technology and institutions that are necessary for future economic growth."

The problems of American business and business organizations are highlighted in the takeover phenomenon of recent years. The wave of takeovers — hostile acquisitions — has a great deal to do with our future economic institutions — our business organizations. The takeovers touch directly on what Americans want — and don't want — in how business is organized and operated in the United States. Takeovers have a bearing on the long-standing American debate over the character of business and its relationship to the communities where it operates.

Beyond question, the takeover fever of recent years has destabilized American business. Famous company names have disappeared because of corporate raids organized by financial operators and speculators. Communities have lost vital payrolls as workers have lost their jobs. Long-serving, responsible managements have been ousted.

Irving Kristol, a member of *The Wall Street Journal* Board of Contributors, offers one of the most incisive criticisms of the takeover fever. He points out that, for the first time in American history, companies have been dismembered "in order to sell off the parts." And he notes that "the debt to equity ratio of American corporations is on the rise as corporation after corporation frantically tries to escape dismemberment."[9] The result of this process is weaker companies and a weaker business sytem for the United States.

The stock market in corporate assets endangers almost every asset-rich corporation. Managements have to look behind them in fear of raiders. Consequently, they cannot afford to take the long view of their company's future prospects, or afford to fund long-range research. This handicaps American business and industry just when national economic success has come to depend more than ever on long-term planning.

Apologists for the corporate raiders say that takeovers lead to more efficient companies; but, the record shows that hostile acquisitions usually are aimed at gutting companies and stripping them of their cash. The present wave of takeovers is fundmentally different than in the past but the apologists do not seem to realize it. Horizontal mergers that aim at greater market share and economies of scale, or mergers that seek the improved coordination and faster "throughput" of vertical integration, do fit the market theories of the apologists — theories that see change in business structure as being motivated by the pursuit of efficiency. The aim of such actions is to build bigger and better engines of production, lower costs translating into larger sales and higher profits. This has long been a basic strength of the American system. Alfred D. Chandler, who has spent a life-time studying the American business system, has said that:

> The firms that first grew large by taking the merger route remained profitable only if after consolidating; they adopted a strategy of vertical integration . . . . By then the visible hand of management replaced the invisible hand of market forces in coordinating the flow from the suppliers of raw materials to the ultimate consumer.[10]

The end result was corporations with the power and position to expand rapidly. It is interesting to note that, just as many analysts today cite the greater size and integration of Japanese corporations compared to American firms as a source of advantage for Tokyo, Chandler cited the greater size and integration of American corporations compared to British firms at the turn of the century when the U.S. surpassed England as the world's leading economic power.

Past merger movements, however, were different from the current takeover binge that aims merely to enrich individual raiders who are financial speculators rather than industrialists. The efficient operation of the firms taken over is not their concern, because they do not intend to operate them, only convert them into quick profits and then move on. This is disintegration, not integration. H. Ross Perot, one of America's most successful businessmen, has stated that "the endless orgies of raids and takeovers has a lot more to do with making large fees and personal profits than with revitalizing corporations."[11] This is pillage, not production.

Irving Kristol cites the basic antagonism between the Wall Street financial community and the American business community. Wall Street, he says, "makes a lot of money out of takeovers and is supremely indifferent to the human and social costs involved." Kristol rightly observes that "a corporation is a sociological institution as well as an aggregation of eocnomic assets."[12] All corporations change with time, but they should change for the right reasons. They should not be changed by what amounts to financial piracy. Corporations have cultivated executive, employee, community and customer loyalty. That has been and should always remain a part of the American free enterprise system. The corporate raiders are undermining the fabric of loyalty and identity upon which the free enterprise system depends.

For that reason, Kristol, among many others, urges legislative action to safeguard companies against the takeover speculators who are not interested in the companies they aim to seize. He would guard against corporate raiders by imposing a "residency requirement" on stockholders, whereby no stockholder would be entitled to a vote until he had held his stock for a year. This would frustrate those who purchase stock in a company for speculative rather than investment purposes.

Happily, a number of states concerned about the fate of longtime, good corporate citizens have enacted anti-takeover legislation. Minnesota, Washington, North Carolina, Massachusetts, Missouri, Florida, Tennessee and Indiana are among the states that have determined that it is in the public interest to thwart corporate raiders. Minnesota, for example, has passed a law to forbid the winner of a hostile takeover from selling any of the company's assets for five years. This type of legislation, designed to safeguard the integrity of industrial organizations, is anathema to the elements in the financial community that profit from dismembering acquired companies. Neal Pierce of *National Journal* says that "In the theology of Wall Street financiers, any value save the cash benefit to shareholders is the rankest damnation."[13] A thoughtful conservative policy to thwart pillaging by the raiders would be a policy geared to the interest of free enterprise and efficient production, not to the false "efficient market" of Wall Street. As Chandler concluded, "Modern business enterprise became a viable institution only after the visible hand of management proved to be more efficient than the invisible hand of market forces in coordinating the flow of materials through the economy."[14]

Not all the states are moving fast enough on this problem, which makes recourse to a nation-wide set of rules enacted by Congress look inviting. However, there is danger in this. The raiders are eager to back a preemptive federal law that would invalidate the state laws. They hope that the federal law would be weaker than the state laws and/or lack the teeth to enforce its provisions. Such a weak bill would not be in the interests of the country or the business community. Action at the state level now provides the best prospects for building defenses against the raiders.

Orderly Markets

In the 1980s, the takeover fever contributed significantly to serious disturbances in the markets, culminating in the stock market crash of October 19, 1987. Christopher Wood of *The Economist* observed that "The sheer scale and speed of the crash clearly made nonsense of yesterday's conventional wisdom that 1929 'could never happen again.'" He said that many younger participants in the financial markets "thought that history was irrelevant."[15]

Investors, as opposed to speculators, should be very mindful of the nation's financial history. They should be supportive of market reforms proposed by the presidentially-appointed Brady Commission, set up after the 1987 crash to investigate and recommend. The reforms proposed would help ensure that the financial security of the United States would not be endangered in the future as it was in 1987. Unfortunately, the changes recommended by the Commission have not been acted upon. The Reagan administration responded to them in a completely negative way. But the country cannot afford to wait until the next crisis hits the markets to energize a public outcry for reform. The Brady Commission report, which restores the focus on investment while making speculation more difficult, should gain strong bipartisan support in Congress in the year ahead.

Louis Lowenstein, Director of the Center for Law and Economics at Columbia University, has pointed out the root problem with the markets, namely that "the line between speculation and investment has been blurred." He referred to the "industry" that has grown up around stock index futures and options as "institutional casinos."[16] In recent years, emphasis has been placed on short-term trading profits instead of long-term returns based on the performance of companies as productive suppliers of goods and services to the public. This perverse emphasis invited the crash. It only created financial "bubbles" rather than solid economic gains. Lowenstein rightly states that "future markets are an ideal breeding ground for speculation."[17] He calls for imposition of margin requirements on such trading and other reforms designed to reduce speculation.

The wise men of American business well understand that it is unconscionable to stonewall on stock market reform. Ross Perot, an advocate of reform, has said, "Any industry which can afford to pay 28-year-old boys $500,000 to $1 million a year for unproductive work on Wall Street sends a signal to the world that its fees are excessive."[18] If rewards are indicative of priorities, the system's priorities are out of kilter. It was because of this and other excesses, Mr. Perot says, that he got out of the stock market before "Black Tuesday" in 1987. "The optimism of the market" he said, "didn't fit the problems of the economy."[19]

Lending Institutions

One of the critical areas of the American economy at this time is its lending institutions. The country has suffered the failure of sizeable banks in recent years. In some states, the failure rate is the highest since the Great Depression. Overall, commercial banking is sound, but a combination of unpayable loans to domestic energy producers and farmers and to the Third World have imposed a heavy strain on banks in several regions. Many banks are on the endangered list. This situation makes it incumbent on banks to adhere firmly to their fiduciary responsibilities.

The most worrisome situation involves the so-called thrift institutions. Freewheeling lending in the early 1980s resulted in the collapse of many Savings and Loans (S&Ls) and threatened the collapse of many others. Almost one thousand S&Ls lost a total of $5.1 billion in the first quarter of 1988. Overall, the industry had a net loss of $3.8 billion.

At this writing, the Federal Savings and Loan Insurance Corporation (FSLIC) lacks the cash to cover losses. Well-managed thrift institutions, which operated in a prudent fashion in the 1980s when other S&Ls were making speculative loans, are now having to pay substantial insurance premium surcharges to the FSLIC to bail out those who were irresponsible. Even then, the surcharges cannot cover the enormous losses. The bailout of just two California S&Ls in June 1988 cost $1.3 billion. Before long, one can be sure that the taxpayers will be called upon to make a multi-billion dollar infusion of funds into the FSLIC. Estimates of the total cost of merging or bailing out insolvent S&Ls range from $36 billion to $80 billion.

Congress cannot ignore this situation indefinitely, though, as in most situations where painful decisions have to be made, it would like to. Almost certainly in 1989 Congress will be forced to tap general revenues to deal with the problem, a disturbing prospect at a time when the budget is already in the red. Depositors are insured up to $100,000 and the promise to cover these deposits has to be honored not only as a contractual obligation but out of economic necessity. The failure of the government (at that time the Federal Reserve Board) to support the banking system and to safeguard depositors accounts at the onset of the Great Depression led to that depression being so deep and lasting so long. But banking system support must not reward reckless officials of sick S&Ls that engaged in speculative ventures and, in effect, "ripped off" their institutions. It would be wrong to reward those who created this costly problem in the first place or to protect them from the consequences of their folly.

For the future, strict accountability, the most conservative accounting rules and a keen sense of fiduciary responsibility — safeguarding other people's money — must characterize all lending institutions in the United States. The painful bailouts that lie ahead should impress these requirements on the public and on every phase of the lending industry.

Insurance Issues

As important as the security of banking and other lending institutions is the stability of the insurance industry. Life, health, property and casualty, and every type of insurance offered by private companies is of central importance to the American people, businesses and non-profit institutions. Life without health insurance providers is unthinkable in our society. Insurance companies also play an immensely important role as a source of funds for constructive investments.

The importance of the insurance industry is often overlooked by legislators and the media. In many states, it is open season on insurance companies. Enormous jury verdicts, including punitive damages, are routine. Irresponsible awards make it all but impossible in some states to provide the insurance coverage people need. The excessive awards of recent years have forced up the cost of some types of insurance to where not only individuals but organizations cannot afford the insurance they need. Today's tort system stifles research and innovation by inhibiting introduction of new products.

Peter W. Huber has written that the average judgment in all tort cases rose from an inflation-adjusted $50,000 in the early 1960s to $250,000 in the early 1980s.[20] Million-dollar judgments are now commonplace. The mushrooming number of attorneys in American society has caused every conceivable type of damage suit to be filed — even damage suits against clergymen alleged to have given hurtful advice. This is "a liability system gone haywire," as Sen. Mitch McConnell of Kentucky has said.[21] Plaintiffs file suits whether a claim has any merit or not in the hopes that the costs of a trial and the risks attending any jury verdict will lead the defendant to settle out of court.

This situation has created a movement to achieve tort reform at the state and federal levels. The reforms are difficult to achieve, however, because plaintiff lawyers are highly-organized, well-funded, and have tremendous clout in Congress and state legislatures, where members are primarily lawyers. There have been victories at the state level, and pressure for tort reform in Congress is growing. It must be reinforced during the next few years if insurance companies are to continue to be able to offer the coverage the public wants and needs.

The filing of frivolous and harassing lawsuits aimed at huge settlements is not the only problem threatening the availability of needed insurance. The attorneys-general of several states have filed a lawsuit against the major insurance companies alleging anti-competitive actions, including the raising of premiums to cover tort abuse. This constitutes political harassment on a major scale. It is thought to be more popular to blame the insurance companies for the problem rather than plaintiffs, their lawyers and indulgent juries. Yet, as every buyer of insurance knows, few industries in the United States can claim to be more competitive than insurance. Not only are there a very large number of insurance companies to choose from, but also myriad independent agents. The anti-competitiveness allegation has been refuted by numerous sources, including the Governor's Advisory Committee on Insurance in New York State, which reported that "We have encountered no evidence to support any assertion that an industry conspiracy or collective manipulation has occurred."[22] The need now is to persuade Congress and the state legislatures that the allegations are unfounded so that a climate conducive to tort reform and to the health of insurance providers and their customers can be created.

Private Pension Plans

Pension plans are part of the total wage and benefits package offered by employers to employees. From the worker's standpoint, pensions are a form of savings. Money that would otherwise be paid in wages or some other form of benefit is invested in a retirement fund. From the firm's standpoint, pensions are used to control worker turnover by building a long-term link between the worker and the firm. They can also be used like any other element of the compensation package as an incentive for improved productivity. They are thus properly left to the private sector, their details to be negotiated by managers and workers.

The federal government has become involved in regulating pension plans. There is justification for this: first, to prevent workers from being defrauded; and second, to reduce the burden on the Pension Benefit Guarantee Corporation (and the taxpayers) by requiring that pension plans be funded so that workers will have their benefits protected against the failure of the company. Unfortunately, the government has sought to expand its control over pensions for two reasons that are unjustified. First, the welfare state mentality of the federal bureaucracy and vote-seeking politicians see pension plans as another opportunity to redistribute money from "wealthy" corporations and higher-income workers to lower-income workers. This is particularly attractive to such officials in a period of tight budgets. It is better, from their perspective, to require private companies to provide and fund mandated benefits than for the government to do so. Thus there are drives to increase benefits at the bottom of the scale and restrict benefits at the top. There have also been measures to shorten the length of time before vesting occurs and to increase portability of benefits between firms. Perhaps most ominous has been the move to eliminate excess asset reversion so that firms cannot withdraw money contributed to a pension plan that exceeds what is needed to fund the plan.

All of these efforts weaken the pension system. By increasing the costs to firms of establishing retirement plans, fewer firms are willing to start new plans and many firms are liquidating established plans. Plans which continue can only do so if the increased costs are met by reducing other elements in the wage/benefit package — elements that most workers would probably value more than redistribution. Prohibiting firms from withdrawing excess funds works as an incentive for firms to underfund their plans since they risk losing any money placed in the fund as a safety margin.

The second reason for pension control stems from Congress' constant search for new sources of revenues. Qualified pension plans cost the government money because their income is exempt from taxation. This "loophole" has attracted the attention of "revenue enhancers." However, to tax the income from retirement plans would again make it less attractive for firms to establish such plans in the first place or to maintain them once the tax was in effect. The government might gain some extra revenue, but fewer workers would be covered by plans. This, in the long run, would increase the burden on the Social Security system. Social Security was established as a supplemental retirement fund, the assumption being that workers would themselves provide the bulk of the money for their retirement. To the extent that workers do not make such provision, the political pressure to increase Social Security benefits grows, and with it the tax burden.

There is also an immediate benefit to the economy from a large and healthy pension private system. Funds committed to such retirement programs become part of the national savings pool available for productive investment. When the government reduces this pool by taxes and regulations that discourage pension plans, the economy suffers a decrease in capital formation, investment and hence the means for growth. Even if taxes did not discourage pension plans, the transfer of funds from investment to the U.S. Treasury would have the same impact, since the bulk of government spending is for public consumption rather than investment in capital goods or infrastructure.

A tax on pension income would be neutral in its effects on the economy only if every dollar taken in taxes reduced the deficit by a dollar and there were no disincentive effects on the creation of pension plans. Neither of those conditions are likely to be met, so it is in the interests of workers and employers, and of the economy as a whole, to have a large and financially-sound private pension system. The federal government must resist the temptation to tinker with the pension system or overburden it in pursuit of goals the system was never intended to fulfill. This means that nearly all of the pension reforms enacted in the 1980s should be repealed and the federal role returned to one of merely serving as a watchdog over the integrity of the system.

Chapter VIII

Resources: The Need for Security and Independence

Energy Independence

A basic need of the United States is to break its dependency on imported oil. The OPEC (1973-74) and Iranian (1979) oil shocks should have impressed the importance of energy independence on national legislators, the administration, opinion leaders and the general public. Even after the recession ended, high oil prices and the risks of new crisis slowed economic growth throughout the decade and represented a massive transfer of wealth to the OPEC countries.

For a time, the problems stemming from import dependency made an impression. Significant steps were taken in the late 1970s and early 1980s to reduce reliance on foreign oil. By 1986, oil imports fell to 31 percent of U.S. consumption. Since then, however, imports have risen sharply to 41 percent in 1987; they may rise to 70 percent or more by the 1990s. Oil imports account for 23 percent of the U.S. trade deficit. The United States imports some 750,000 barrels per day from Saudi Arabia.

Without adequate incentives for drilling and so-called "cheap" oil available from abroad, U.S. production was dropping by 150,000 to 200,000 barrels per day per year by mid-1988. *Barron's* estimated that the U.S. would soon require an increase in imports of 200,000 to 400,000 barrels per day each year.[1] Understandably, OPEC is rejoicing.

Americans need to be aware of the danger in not seeking energy independence. By importing four out of every ten barrels it consumes, the United States exposes itself to another threat of a crippling embargo. At the time of the 1973-74 embargo, the United States was importing approximately half its oil, a situation the country is again approaching. Moreover, there is a steadily-increasing use of petroleum for things other than energy. Car bodies and many auto parts are made from oil, as is polyester in clothing, paving materials, fibers in carpets, bottles, aircraft equipment and even toothpaste tubes.

The upward course of oil imports has to be arrested and then reversed if the United States is to enjoy economic security. Today, motorists and other oil users are supplied by Saudi Arabia, Mexico, Kuwait, Trinidad and other nations with current or potential problems. Many of the large oil companies continue to rely on oil imports. Texaco, for example, buys more crude oil from Saudi Arabia than does any nation except the United States.

Though the country has taken steps to diversify its sources of imports, the fact that the oil market is global means that disruptions anywhere in the market will impact on all importers by reducing the availability and raising the price on the world market. When one considers not just the immediate dollar cost of imported oil, but the instability to the economy and the risk of war that imports represent, it is clear to see that energy dependence is extremely expensive.

Energy dependency is increasing in other ways. Foreign interests, including state-owned firms, are buying into American oil fields and refineries. Kuwait owns 22 percent of an Alaskan oil field. Saudi Arabia is trying to buy refineries on the Texas coast at bargain prices to exploit the depression in that area. Other major oil companies have partial foreign ownership. All of this adds up to diminished U.S. control over even its own domestic oil supplies, and hence its economic destiny. Will the U.S. government be free to make significant foreign policy moves in the Middle East and elsewhere if a substantial portion of its oil industry and related facilities is under foreign ownership and control? It is only reasonable to answer that question in the negative. Economic control leads to political power. If foreigners could simultaneously dispute both imports and domestic U.S. oil supplies, the damage would make the incidents of the 1970s look minor in comparison.

Restoration of incentives for drilling and repeal of the windfall profits tax will be necessary in order to revive the domestic oil industry and stimulate new exploration. But those measures, by themselves, will not suffice to move the country once again in the direction of energy independence. Numerous students of the problem are convinced that the best — perhaps the only — way to achieve the national security goal of energy independence is to enact a variable import fee on all oil brought into the United States. This would raise the price of imported oil and, in the judgement of William Safire, conservative columnist for *The New York Times*, result in "conserving energy and using less oil from overseas." Safire also argues that a $10 per barrel fee would "slash the budget deficit by some $23 billion a year."[2] This approach to the situation should receive the considered attention of Congress and the new administration.

Coal and Minerals

As disturbing as the oil situation is, there is also a growing American reliance on imported coal and strategic minerals. Because of deindustrialization, the drop in imported oil prices and the availability of foreign coal produced by cheap labor, American coal mining from Pennsylvania to North Dakota has suffered. Mines have been shut down and production has been reduced. Further reductions are likely when existing contracts with large coal users expire. Already available and being imported are millions of tons of coal from Colombia — coal produced from mines developed by Exxon. In addition, Armand Hammer, who has a history of business dealings with communist regimes, has entered his Occidental Petroleum company into a joint venture with the People's Republic of China to open a $800 million coal mine in North China. This new, low-cost coal, mined under what by American standards are intolerable conditions, presents a serious threat to U.S. coal producers, their employees and home states unless a national policy is established that safeguards American interests.

American coal mines in the northern tier of states are also in trouble because of imported electricity from Canada. Canadian power production is government-subsidized and eliminates utility customers vital to American coal producer states such as North

Dakota. This situation again illustrates the absence of a national energy policy.

Low-cost production abroad has also played havoc with other American mineral producers. Foreign producers pay wages that are a tiny fraction of those in the United States. U.S. companies cannot mine ores at the same cost, nor can U.S. companies compete with foreign producers who do not have to abide by environmental laws like those in this country. The absence of environmental protection regulations in Mexico is the main reason that the United States has lost its once sizeable smelter industry. These facts again demonstrate how free trade rewards irresponsible and antisocial behavior by foreign firms and governments.

U.S. government policy forbids importing rare strategic minerals from South Africa. But strategic minerals such as platinum are not readily available elsewhere and cannot be found in the United States. Despite its internal problems, South Africa still has a government that would like to cooperate with the United States. The irony of Congress' sanctions legislation against South Africa is that America is now forced to shift its purchases of a number of strategic "exotic" minerals vital to high-technology and national defense to the only other large scale producer: the Soviet Union, America's most dangerous adversary. In a future period of confrontation with the Soviet Union, the United States would find itself in a very vulnerable position if it depended on the Soviets for vital imports.

Sound public policy should dictate the safeguarding of domestic mineral production, the development of alternatives where possible for imports, and a return to reliance on friendly governments in Africa for rare metals not available in North America. The U.S. National Defense Stockpile of strategic metals should be expanded to cushion any supply disruption. Unfortunately, in recent years, the federal government has been reducing these stockpiles in a short-sighted attempt to generate revenues during a time of large budget deficits. The amount of money involved in maintaining these stockpiles is small relative to the budget, whereas the stockpiles are quite valuable as a reserve to the economy. Should there be a crisis, prices will jump if the minerals are available at all. Now is the time to add to the reserves.

Imports as a Percentage of Domestic Use: Strategic Metals[3]

Imports over 90 percent
Titanium (1, 2, 3)
Aluminum and Bauxite (9)
Tantalum (5, 6, 7)
Manganese (1, 6)
Cobalt (2, 8, 9)
Chromium (1, 2, 3)
Platinum Group (1, 2, 8)
Fluorine (1, 4)
Tin (7, 9)
Diamond (1, 8)
Columbium (NA)
Mica (6, 9)
Strontium (4, 8)

Imports over 75 percent
Nickel (5, 8, 9)
Germanium-Indium (NA)
Tungsten (NA)
Asbestos (1, 5)

Imports over 50 percent
Berylium (NA)
Zirconium (NA)
Cadmium (4, 5, 8)
Zinc (4, 5, 8)
Potassium (5, 8)
Selenium (4, 5, 8)

Supplier Codes: 1 = South Africa; 2 = other southern Africa, 3 = USSR, 4 = Mexico, 5 = Canada, 6 = Brazil, 7 = Thailand, 8 = Europe, 9 = other Third World

The same logic holds for the Strategic Petroleum Reserve. The Reserve was increased during the first part of the decade, but again, as with the mineral stockpiles, budget pressures have brought the project to a halt. When prices are low and the oil is flowing, few people worry about the reserve supply. Yet, this is precisely when reserves can be built up at the least cost. Thinking about the Reserve when trouble hits is too late. The government should make its purchases for the Reserve from domestic oil producers so as to stimulate the American oil indusry and bring some relief to the depressed economies of the oil-producing states.

Resource-Based States

The oil, coal and mineral-producing states have tremendous importance to the American economy and to its strategic position in the world. With the emphasis on growth in the consumer sectors of the economy, however, the basic role of the producer states has been neglected. The booming economies on the Pacific and Mid-Atlantic coasts have masked the depression that has gripped industry, energy, minerals and agriculture in the American heartland. Too many policymakers have considered these states to be expendable.

This attitude is an outgrowth of the notion that the United States now has a "post-industrial" economy and can therefore afford to abandon the elements that sustain an industrial economy. It is hard to conceive of a more mistaken view of the world. No matter how sophisticated and advanced American technology becomes, its foundation will still consist of the material ingredients of manufacturing, food and fibers. Despite the talk of an economy based on information, communications and software, none of these can provide the basics of food, shelter and clothing or the myriad of other material goods Americans crave. They are adjuncts to production, not replacements for production.

A generation ago, there was a regular, systematic review of U.S. industrial capabilities and their supporting resources. Dr. John Ellison, former dean of the Industrial College of the Armed Forces, has pointed out that the review function was performed through the 1950s by the Munitions Board and the National Security Resources Board.[4] It might be well for the U.S. government to restore the National Security Resources Board and give it a broad mandate. This function could also be incorporated in the enlarged economics sector of a reformed National Security Council, as outlined earlier.

It is important to help balance the economies of resource-rich states. This could be accomplished by means of a clear-cut national policy of decentralizing government research facilities and other installations. At this time, America's research facilities are unduly concentrated in a handful of areas. The entire country, however, has a stake in encouraging technological development in lightly-populated states as well as heavily-populated ones. Moreover, many of the uncrowded heartland states maintain the work ethic of an earlier period and do not have the social problems, crime and ideological alienation that has become characteristic of the congested, urban areas. In many of the less-populated areas, there are also extensive opportunities for joint project-sharing among several states or establishment of regional compacts to accomplish specific tasks.

R. Scott Fosler, vice president of the Committee for Economic Development in Washington, D.C., has urged regional development for the American heartland in the light of the "weakened ability of federal macroeconomic policy to guide the U.S. economy." He notes that the 13 heartland states — Kansas, Colorado, Iowa, Arkansas, Minnesota, Missouri, Montana, Nebraska, New Mexico, North and South Dakota, Oklahoma and Wyoming — are the states heavily dependent on natural resource industries, agriculture, oil, gas and tourism.[5]

Maintaining and supporting development across national territories is a concern in countries from Great Britain to Canada. Excessive concentration of population and facilities is widely regarded as unwise. One of the most notable examples of foreign efforts along these lines is the development of the eastern provinces of the USSR over the last twenty years. As Rodger Swearingen, a professor of international relations at the University of Southern California, has noted, "The economic and strategic development of Siberia and the Soviet Far East marks the metamorphosis of the Soviet Union from a European to a world power."[6] The Soviets have made huge investments in infrastructure and industry — particularly heavy metallurgy — in these resource-rich areas known for their oil, coal, nickel, tin, aluminum, lead, zinc, timber and gold. The ironic part of this is that while the United States has been unable or unwilling to invest in the revitalization of its resource/industrial heartland, Soviet development has been underwritten by an influx of Western capital and technology. There is little question, Dr. Swearingen says, that:

> ... high-technology transfer from the West has played a significant role in the region's economic and strategic development. Without European, Japanese, American and other Western technology, systematically secured (legally or otherwise) over a period of several decades, the striking rail-communications complex, industrial development, oil and gas pipelines, Pacific seaport construction and related strategic process — if possible at all in the near term — would have taken considerably longer to achieve.[7]

It is a sad commentary on American policy that no such undertakings have been launched in the United States even though the means to do so are readily available. What is lacking is the "zeal, ingenuity and creativity" which Swearingen sees the Soviets exhibit towards resource/industrial development. These attributes are supposed to belong to capitalist societies.

In the United States, regional disparities have weakened the country in the past, as when the southern states were grossly deficient in modernization and affluence between the end of the Civil War and the coming of World War II. The American constitutional system is a system of states; the national interest lies in strengthening the economic and social fabric of the entire system and each individual state. If certain states were to become losers in national development on a major scale and turn into virtual shells of their former selves, the situation might well encourage tampering with the fundamental political structure of the United States.

Electric Power

In many ways, the electric power industry is our most basic industry. No business or industry can operate without abundant electricity. Certainly, a nation that believes itself to be in a computer-based information age should be concerned about the availability of electric power.

Happily, the U.S. electric power industry enjoys general good health. It is innovative and looks to the future. However, there is reason to be concerned whether the growing electric power needs of the country will be met. The United States pioneered the use of atomic energy and it once had a monopoly on the construction of nuclear power plants. The nuclear power industry has built plants in America that are unrivaled in efficiency and safety. Today, however, the United States is in retreat from the nuclear age. Anti-nuclear extremists have been successful in blocking new power reactor construction. They have delayed the completion of plants such as the Seabrook reactor in New Hampshire. They have harassed railroads that ship nuclear materials for storage. They have thwarted plans to develop nuclear waste disposal sites. In the case of the Long Island Shoreham plant, they have succeeded in getting the Governor of New York to manipulate the web of rules that regulate federal-state relations in such a way that a completed $5 billion reactor complex will now be scrapped. This is a nuclear plant that is much needed by the residents and commercial users of electricity on Long Island. It is because of this campaign that the prospects for nuclear energy and the nuclear equipment industry in the United States are so dismal. Anti-nuclear reaction seems to have won the day, forcing the United States into a posture that will handicap the nation in the decades ahead.

While the anti-nuclear radicals have waged their campaign against modern technology in the United States, nuclear power generation has surged ahead in other countries. France is the Western leader in building nuclear generating plants, having made the commitment twenty years ago to fulfill all future electricity demands with nuclear power. Over 55 percent of France's electricity now comes from the atom. Japan, like France, is well aware that importing oil from distant sources makes it vulnerable. In response, Tokyo has undertaken a very extensive nuclear construction program. There are vocal anti-nuke movements in some of these countries, movements which have often turned to violence, but their governments have been wise enough to dismiss the noise of the protesters and proceed in the general interest of progress. The U.S. government seems to lack both the wisdom and the courage to do the same. Yet, if a comprehensive plan for energy development is not undertaken, by the mid-1990s the United States will find itself, despite its greater domestic resource endowments, as dependent on oil imports as Japan.

Japanese and U.S. Energy Use Compared[8]
(percent of total energy consumed by source)

	Japan's Energy Plan				U.S. actual
	1977	1985	1990	1995	1985
Domestic Oil	—	—	—	—	24.8
Imported Oil	75.0	63.0	50.0	45.0	19.8
Coal	14.8	16.1	17.8	18.3	24.4
Nuclear Power	2.0	6.7	10.9	14.3	9.4
Natural Gas	2.9	7.2	9.0	8.7	18.4
Hydroelectric/ Solar/other	0.1	1.3	6.5	9.4	3.4

Japan plans to shift 15.8 percent of its energy consumption from imported oil to nuclear and coal-fired power plants. Unlike Japan, America has abundant coal supplies, and it could eliminate the need to import oil altogether if it adopted the same kind of plan as Tokyo has devised.

The Soviet Union, of course, continues its nuclear construction. The Chernobyl nuclear reactor accident has led to new designs, not new fears. Ironically, the Chernobyl accident has done more to cripple the U.S. nuclear program than the Soviet, despite the fact that American reactors are far more advanced and protected than was the obsolete Chernobyl facility.

The United States should renew its commitment to the nuclear age. Congress and the president must arrive at a pro-nuclear power consensus. It must be made clear that the United States will not fall behind Third World regimes in the development of nuclear power generation. Restarting the nuclear power program is essential for the American people in light of the nation's growing dependency on imported energy supplies. If nuclear efforts had been carried forward at a proper pace since the 1970s, the United States would not be as energy dependent as it is today.

A renewed commitment means a decision to accelerate the licensing process, to push aside frivolous and obstructionist efforts to delay nuclear construction. Such delaying tactics were established in the early 1970s to make nuclear plants financially unviable. Costs are driven up directly by elaborate and redundant safety and environmental regulations; delays impose heavy capital and interests costs and increase construction and labor costs. The average U.S. nuclear plant takes twice as much time and money to build as the average French plant.

The record clearly shows that nuclear power is the safest form of energy generation. Unable to prove their wild scare claims against nuclear technology, the anti-nuclear radicals have resorted to strangling projects with red tape. It is the bureaucracy, not that technology, that is defective. It should be the target of sweeping reform.

Samuel McCracken was a Senior Research Fellow at Boston University's Center for Energy before becoming a scientific advisor to President Reagan. He has argued that:

... nuclear energy, far from being a pariah among resources, ought to be the energy source of choice for all uses for which electricity is a suitable intermediary. It does not matter whether electric generators waste heat if they waste heat derived from abundant and otherwise useless thorium. Waste is, after all, the misuse of something that could be better used otherwise. On the long haul, any use of oil to generate electricity is entirely waste. But thorium, essentially incapable of being used elsewhere, can be wasted only through disuse. The same is true for uranium and plutonium ....[9]

Thorium is the principle fuel in the new High-Temperature Gas-Cooled Reactor (HTGR). It is estimated that the world supply of thorium represents more potential energy than all coal, oil and natural gas reserves combined.

It must be recognized that anti-nuclearism is only part of a larger campaign that opposes the construction and advancement of all types of power generation. The same zealots who protest against nuclear power one day will be out protesting against off-shore oil drilling the next, or against the use of microwave transmissions (the key to space-based solar power generation) or against the pollution from coal-fired power plants. As individuals, they are as accustomed to turning on their stereo systems, air-conditioners and personal computers as are others in the population. But as a movement, they hypocritically oppose all new power generating units essential to homes, offices, factories, hospitals and other facilities dependent on electrical power.

America cannot afford to indulge such radical and destructive political activism as practiced by the anti-energy movement. New sources of electric power cannot be created overnight. The construction of new power plants, nuclear or fossil-fuel, involves a lead time of years. Utilities have to weigh escalating construction costs, unstable markets and the attitudes of rate-setting agencies. Failure to act today will mean future shortages and higher utility bills.

Acid Rain

Another serious threat to the American electrical power industry and the economy it serves is the acid rain controversy. This has become an international issue dividing the United States and Canada.

For years, Canadian officials and some American environmentalists have charged that sulfur dioxide and oxides of nitrogen are producing acid rain on a large scale. This phenomenon then causes massive damage to lakes, forests and crops in Canada and the northeastern United States. Statements by environmental activists and their zealous supporters in the media have made acid rain appear to be a nightmare.

In 1987, the Interagency National Acid Precipitation Program (INAPP) made public a study based on a long-range assessment of the acid rain problem. The study showed that there was little evidence that there was any substantial threat to the environment or to public health from acid rain. According to *The Wall Street Journal*, the four-volume study, totaling about 925 pages, is "the most thorough examination of acid rain every published." The interagency study said that research has shown that damage to lakes is limited to a few areas and that even in those areas, only a small percentage of the lakes were affected. It repudiates the notion that pollutants from power plants are ruining the environment. In addition, the report said that, in the affected areas, "a significant increase in the number of acidic lakes is unlikely to occur over the next few decades." The report also found little damage to forests or crops and "no demonstrated effects on health from acid rain."[10]

Unfortunately, the Canadians do not care to hear the message contained in such scientific studies. Canada's environment minister simply repeated the unsubstantiated but popular allegations his department had made earlier. Canada's position, however, is untenable given that country's lack of environmental controls such as scrubbers on power company stacks. Canada takes no account of the environmental gains scored in the United States in recent years. The Clean Air Act is working and will have a substantial impact in the years to come. It is noteworthy that sulfur dioxide emissions have decreased 26 percent between 1973 and 1984 and that further reductions will be achieved in the future.

The Canadian demands for a U.S.-funded solution to acid rain are unreasonable. The United States cannot afford to spend billions of dollars to solve a problem that does not exist. Funds devoted to unnecessary, non-productive projects means that these funds are not available for investments that would make the U.S. economy more efficient, expand production capacity and create new jobs. If the United States appeases the Canadians on the acid rain issue, it will mean higher electricity costs for businesses and homeowners.

With the INAPP scientific study in hand, Congress does not need "to do something" simply to make the Canadians or the anti-energy movement happy. The critics of acid rain on both sides of the border must acknowledge that their demands are based on insufficient scientific research.

Chapter IX

Obsolete Labor Organizations

Labor Unions and the Economy

The character of the organized labor movement has changed greatly. From a high of 34 percent in the mid-1950s, the unionized portion of the labor force has declined to less than 18 percent. It is likely that the union percentage will continue to fall as younger Americans, who see little that is useful or attractive in unionism, enter the workforce. The growing number of women in the workforce has also found little of interest in unions.

There is, however, one area where unionism has increased its strength: public employment. There, the percentage has steadily risen, especially among municipal workers and public school teachers. About one-third of total union membership today is made up of public employees. The number of strikes by these public workers is not inconsiderable.

Each new school year features teacher strikes in school districts across the nation. Though teachers on the picket lines claim that they are striking for "quality education," their demands turn out to be the same as unions everywhere: more money for less work. When it comes to real efforts to improve education, the National Education Association (NEA), the largest teacher's union, opposes virtually every reform proposal, particularly those that would ensure competent teaching, high academic standards and rewards based on performance.

NEA has been in the forefront of the radicalization of education.

Social studies has become "a grab bag of current events, ersatz social science, one-worldism and opinion-mongering by uninformed children and half-informed adults," to use the words of Chester E. Finn, Jr., an assistant secretary of education in the Reagan administration. Finn cites Prof. Jan Tucker of Florida International University, an influential educator who has told teachers that the "territorial state" which "depends upon the direct control of territory and military strength to provide security and well-being for its citizens" is an archaic concept that must be driven from the minds of students and replaced with the idea of "global interdependence." Similar views are held by James A. Banks who writes classroom manuals for teachers. Banks tells teachers to abandon the "traditional" approach with its "development of a tenacious and non-reflective nationalism" in favor of an "identification with the global community."[1]

Given the vital importance of education not only to students trying to acquire the skills to succeed but to the entire country trying to stay ahead in a global economic-technological competition, the United States cannot afford schools run by political activists and teachers who are more loyal to their union than to their community. It is not merely a coincidence that while unionism is spreading among teachers, the level of academic achievement was falling among students.

The need to curb disruptive actions aimed at public services must be emphasized anew, not only to ensure open schools but also functioning hospitals and operating police, fire, sanitation and emergency services. Public employees cannot enjoy the same right to engage in strike actions that is enjoyed by employees in the private sector. The public and private sectors are fundamentally different. Private business firms and their employees operate in a competitive environment. If a strike makes one brand of goods unavailable or if wage settlements push prices too high for one company, consumers can turn to another source for the affected items. However, public services are usually monopolies. The government is the only source. A disruption of services impacts fully on the population. Making matters worse, the reason that governments run certain services is because they are so important to public health or safety. They are public to ensure that they are always available. For unions to move into the public sector, as they have, complete contradicts this philosophy of government service.

The private employer also deserves greater legal protection against unions that are hoodlum-controlled or dominated by organized crime, unions where violence is a frequent occurrence against employers and employees alike who are unwilling to cooperate. A Congressional majority should be willing to acknowledge the role of organized crime in certain unions, and the industries in which these unions exercise enormous power despite long records of criminal convictions. Americans cannot be said to enjoy full freedom until the gangster elements are rooted out of unions and brought to justice.

One of the few effective tools available to law enforcement is application of the RICO (Racketeer-Influence Corrupt Organizations) Act. This Act makes it possible to place corrupt, gangster-ruled unions under trustees who will strive towards the reestablishment of democracy in the affected union. Unfortunately, the RICO Act has been applied in only a few cases. The recent effort of Congress to repeal it is disturbing, as is the petition signed by a majority of members of the House of Representatives opposing the use of the RICO Act against the Teamster's Union, perhaps the most notorious union in the country. It is in the public interest that the Justice Department in June 1988 invoked the RICO Act against the Teamsters. Some modification of the law is necessary, however, to prevent its misuse against respectable business.

Congress must also remove the antitrust exemption enjoyed by unions under provision of the Sherman Act. As the law is written today, there is a double standard: businesses are not allowed to combine to inhibit commerce or to conspire to raise prices, but unions are allowed to engage in such harmful activity. Unions have long exercised a constitutionally and socially unacceptable power to interfere with lawful commerce, halting work on docks, railroads, airlines and construction projects and disrupting the production of a wide variety of goods and services. These activities, often involving lawless and violent incidents, could be terminated if the unions were denied exemption under the antitrust law.

Unionism has been defended on the grounds that it helps poor, downtrodden workers gain a larger piece of the pie. Yet the history of unions in America does not support this notion. Unions have generally only been successful in industries with high productivity and which used skilled labor and/or were in strategic fields with economic "leverage." This is because a union cannot gain for its members wages and benefits out of thin air. It can only be successful in a field that is prosperous. But the union acts to erode the prosperity of the industry it has penetrated, leading eventually to the decline of both the industry and the union. It does this with higher wages that raise prices, lower output and reduce employment; with work rules that decrease productivity; and with resistance to innovation. Princeton labor economist Albert Rees has concluded:

> If the union is viewed solely in terms of its effect on the economy, it must in my opinion be considered an obstacle to the optimum performance of our economic system. It alters the wage structure in a way that impedes the growth of employment in sectors of the economy where productivity and income are naturally high and that leaves too much labor in low-income sectors of the economy like southern agriculture and the least skilled service trades . . . and while some of this gain may be at the expense of the owners of capital, most of it must be at the expense of consumers and the lower-paid workers.[2]

The growth of unions in government employment provides a perfect example. Government has been growing, financing itself by taxes and debt at will. Its white-collar workforce, on average, well exceeds the general populace in income and fringe benefits. Because it is government, it is shielded from the discipline of the market. There is no incentive to curb costs, except whatever pressure the voters can exert at election time, which is at best an indirect method of influencing the unelected civil service bureaucracy.

Labor Law Reform

The decline of the American rail system has been a national tragedy. There has been a small revival in recent years in the form of new shortline railroads. However, the rail workers unions are seeking to cripple these new small rail lines, many operated in conjunction with local governments, by saddling them with the same labor rules and practices imposed on larger, long-haul lines. These short lines are vital to many small communities, but they cannot bear the imposition of unreasonable costs, delays and disruptions, and other inefficiencies created by unions. The Railway Labor Act, passed in 1926, permits featherbedding and holds railroads to other outdated work practices while also burdening them with excessive financial requirements. The Act should be amended so that progress in the railroad industry is no longer considered illegal.

The burdens imposed on the trucking industry are of the same basic characteristic as those imposed on the railroads. Trucking companies have to deal with the Teamsters Union which, as already noted, is rightly regarded as one of the most corrupt and hoodlum-dominated unions in the country.

Labor law has tended to support unions, giving them a power they would not otherwise be able to exercise on their own. One can argue that the modern union movement in the United States was created when the government established the National Labor Relations Board (the Wagner Act) in 1935. Ironically, the NLRB was upheld by the Supreme Court in 1937 on the grounds that it would *decrease* the disruption of the economy by unions. The idea was that once unions were recognized and made secure, they would be less militant. That strikes increased by an order of magnitude during the decade following the NLRB's establishment proves that the effect was just the opposite.

Public reaction to union abuses led to the amendment of the NLRB in 1947 (the Taft-Hartley Act). Most of the reforms were made to protect workers from coercion by union bosses. Among the changes was an attempt to strengthen the rights of workers not to join a union if they so desired. This "right to work" provision was made conditional, however, by the inclusion in Section 7 of the phrase "except to the extent that such right may be effected by an agreement requiring union membership as a condition of employment." In other words, if the union can gain a closed ship by contract with a firm, the individual worker loses his rights. This is an intolerable infringement on the civil liberties of every employee. The right of an individual not to join a union should be considered as well-protected under the Constitution and the labor laws as the right of a worker to join a union. Though several states have enacted right to work laws, a true national right to work must become the law of the land.

The Minimum Wage

Unions are the main driving force behind efforts to increase the minimum wage law, not because union members are paid the minimum wage set by statute (union members make far more than this), but because the unions know that the minimum wage is used as the "floor" upon which entire negotiated wage structures are built. By raising the floor, unions hope to raise the levels they are on as well. If such a tactic is successful it will represent another income transfer from lower-paid workers to union members, as well as increased unemployment throughout the economy.

It is an elementary principle of economics that raising the price of any commodity by fiat means that less of it will be used. Applied to labor, this means that wage increases unrelated to productivity increases will lead to higher unemployment. The distinguished economist Thomas Sowell has written:

> The term "minimum wage" law defines the process by its hoped for results. But the law itself does not guarantee that any wage will be paid, because employment remains a voluntary transaction. All that the law does is reduce the set of options available.... What is perhaps most surprising is the persistence and scope of belief that people can be made better off by reducing their options. In the case of the so-called minimum wage law, the empirical evidence has been growing that it not only increases unemployment, but that it does so most among the most disadvantaged workers.[3]

This is because employment depends on a comparison of wages with productivity. Those who are least productive, due to lack of skills, experience or work discipline, will be those who lose their jobs as mandated wage rates move beyond what their labor is worth to prospective employers. The effect of a higher real minimum wage will be to expand the "unemployable" underclass with the predictable effects on welfare costs and crime rates.

The minimum wage has not been raised since 1977. The best strategy for reducing the adverse effect of the minimum wage, short of repealing it completely, is to allow its real rate to continue to be lowered by inflation until it finally becomes irrelevant.

Unions Growing Desperate

As unions have retreated in recent years, a new strategy has been devised by union militants. This is the so-called "corporate campaign" whereby a local dispute is transformed into a national issue. The union targets outside directors on a company's board and endeavor to bring financial and media pressure on these directors' own companies. Here and there this strategy has worked, but it has also failed, most conspicuously against the Hormel Company in Minnesota.[4] The "corporate campaign" is enormously disruptive to the workers involved and to the communities where the targeted plants are hit. Communities and the citizens are whipped into a frenzy, with emotional confrontations that leave lasting divisions. Since media attention is crucial to this union strategy, violence is often used to attract national press coverage. This strategy is fresh evidence of the labor movement's lack of concern for the public interest.

A more subtle campaign, an effort to deal with the serious image problem unions have acquired for themselves over the years, is to move into more middle class and "family" issues. Unions have focused attention on parental leave, mandated social benefits and various health issues. This strategy has been much more successful. However, the old economic realities persist. Whether unions aim for higher wages or high benefits, the result is the same: fewer jobs and weaker industries. Unions are exhibiting, in overt form, the same malady that has infected most of an American society hooked on instant consumption, leisure and debt: the desire to consume more than is being produced. This is a dead end.

As the union movement shrinks, its radical fringe comes to assume greater influence on the remains. Though traditional union leaders are pushing middle-class and family values in an attempt to lure back workers, particularly women, they are losing ground within the labor movement to left-wing activists with an anti-family political agenda that includes joint campaigns with lesbian and "gay rights" groups and an anti-American foreign policy agenda of U.S. disarmament and support for communist regimes. As we move into the 1990s, it will become increasingly apparent that unions have little if anything to contribute to America's progress.

Mandated Benefits

A new term, "mandated benefits," came into general use during the last Congress. One can be sure that it will continue to be heard very often during the next four years. The idea is that employers should be required to provide a wide range of new benefits to employees, including parental leave and more comprehensive health care. Some mandated benefits have already been enacted into law and others will be pushed very hard in the next Congress.

Citizens have to ask themselves: why the demand now for mandating these benefits, imposing their costs on employers? The answer is that the proponents of these benefits lack the political will or ability to have them enacted as government programs, with their costs imposed openly on the taxpayers. They know that the taxpayers would rebel. Therefore, a backdoor and unfair method is proposed to shift the burden onto business. It is an old practice for politicians to seek the credit for new programs while hiding the costs from the public. The politicians gain the votes of special interests without losing votes from the taxpayers.

For decades, this was done by use of deficit spending. The welfare state was based on the notion that expensive entitlement programs could be financed without overt tax increases. Deficits and covert tax increases — the impact of inflation on a progressive tax system — would provide the funds without alarming the public with the cost. Today, however, the government has taken deficit spending as far as it dares, and the public is opposed to higher taxes. So, the politicians see business as the means by which new programs can be enacted without direct costs to the public.

There is no such thing as a free lunch. Somebody pays for everything. Where will business get the money to pay for these expensive new benefits? There are only two sources. The firm can seek to avoid the costs, which are tied to employment, by reducing their covered workforce. Jobs will be eliminated. Or, firms can collect increased revenues to pay for the increased costs by raising prices. Such price increases should rightly be seen by the public as a tax increase.

However, due to increased foreign competition, the ability of firms to pass on cost increases via higher prices is limited. Cost-cutting will be the primary response to new mandated benefits, and this means higher unemployment. Firms will either operate with smaller workforces, increasing the work load on those who remain, or will substitute machines for people since machines do not have to be paid benefits. The effect will be a redistribution of income. Some workers will benefit, but others will lose everything. The marginal gains for those who benefit are not sufficient to justify the large losses suffered by those who will find themselves out of work.

The benefits that Congress wants to enact, if truly desired by workers, are proper subjects for negotiations between employers and employees over compensation. That various special interest groups have turned to Congress to impose these benefits and thus alter compensation packages by law strongly implies that economic conditions are not conducive to the establishment of these benefits in the private sector. Passing a law will not make economic conditions any better. Any attempt to force costs on business which they cannot afford to pay will only lead to further declines in the nation's economic strength and competitiveness.

The whole notion of mandated benefits is that business firms have some hidden pot of gold from which endless new demands can be met. This is nonsense. Firms only have the money they collect from their customers through voluntary transactions. Then they must manage their proceeds in the best way possible. Government attempts to reallocate these funds by fiat will only disrupt the system.

Chapter X

America's Heritage: The Foundation on Which to Rebuild

Social Issues

The business community, for its part, cannot afford to concentrate solely on economic issues and leave social concerns untouched. Business has to be alert to changing patterns of life and the need to undergird the family. A good employee is one who is solidly rooted in his or her community and is confident that society is mindful of his family's needs. Business must continue to play a major leadership role in the communities where it operates and to support efforts to deal with problems such as pornography and drugs that infest so many American cities and towns. Responsible, efficient workers are those who are not only well-schooled but also securely grounded in basic American values. The work ethic has to be constantly reinforced if American business and industry are to compete in the years ahead. And, understanding of the work ethic and of good citizenship begins in the home.

A new emphasis on community is a proper feature of business conservatism in the future. Industrial society in the 20th century often has been destructive of community. Business frequently finds it necessary to relocate facilities or to move employees to new plants in distant parts of the country. Much of this is inevitable, given the need for factories and offices to be located with ready access to raw materials, labor, transportation and markets. But the long-range interest of the American business system — the free enterprise system — is in minimizing change that is harmful to the sense of community. People with a strong sense of place are likely to have a stronger sense of loyalty to the company for which they work. This is an important value to preserve. Just as it is said that patriotism is rooted in loyalty to one's family, there is a seamless web of relationships that business needs to be part of. Business leaders must remember that people are not so much committed to free enterprise as an abstract theory as they are to a particular company or profession in which they see their own personal future and the future of their family fulfilled. When relocation is essential, a company surely will find it a matter of enlightened self-interest to help build a new community feeling, a bond between a place to live and a place to work.

The Battle Over Western Civilization

Though Congress has passed major immigration legislation, including a controversial amnesty provision for many persons who entered the United States illegally, one can be sure that immigration will be considered again by Congress in the next few years. Basic principles governing immigration need to be set forth and fully understood by Congress, federal officials and the public.

In a fundamental sense, immigration remains out of control, despite the new law or perhaps because of it and its amnesty provision. No one can reasonably assert that the tide of illegal immigrants has ebbed. Illegals continue to enter the United States across our long, largely undefended, southern border. It has been established that these illegals come from Mexico and other Central American and Caribbean countries and from as far away as Hong Kong and Bangladesh. The world knows that the U.S. border is virtually an open border, its southern boundary a line separating an affluent, advanced nation from a poverty-stricken region of the Third World. Is it any wonder that the flood of immigrants grows higher every year? Or that problems result? The flow will surely continue to rise unless the United States acts to change its image as an easy mark. After all, the world knows that America has granted blanket amnesty for illegals. Given this precedent and continued weak law enforcement, the expectations are that it will yield its sovereignty again and again.

The United States has the most liberal legal immigration policy in the world. There is also a large flow of immigrants from Southeast Asia and elsewhere who enter the country under special legislation, particularly refugee legislation. This has given some American cities almost a Third World character. To be sure, many refugees have settled into communities and have scored important accomplishments in work and education. On the other hand, the sheer number of newcomers has had a profoundly unsettling effect in some cities, and the problems involved in bringing newcomers into the mainstream of America's social and political culture are acute.

The illegal immigration from Mexico and elsewhere in Latin America has been so extensive that educational, health and welfare services have been overwhelmed. Cities near the Mexican border face staggering financial burdens in caring for the needs of the new immigrants, those legal, illegal and here because of the amnesty provision. The American Immigration Control Foundation, quoting a study by Prof. Donald Huddle of Rice University, reports that illegal aliens double the jobless rate among working Americans and that unemployment costs are increased by $35 billion a year.[1]

The overall problem is compounded because the process of Americanization today is far less effective than it was in the early years of the century. Then, immigrants, primarily from Europe, eagerly sought to learn and embrace the traditional values of the United States. Now, only one of every ten immigrants to the United States is from Europe. This makes the cultural gap between the new immigrants and American society far greater than at the opening of the century.

Crossing the gap is made difficult by radical groups that seek to perpetuate a kind of foreign self-segregation in the midst of American society. The demand for bilingual education is very strong; such a system would introduce the kind of dual culture that has so disrupted Canadian life. In Canada, the French-speaking minority requires the English-speaking majority to use French as a second official language, while refusing to use English itself. This seems to be the trend in many parts of the United States with regard to Spanish. Yet, just as we have discovered that racial segregation is harmful, we see cultural and linguistic segregation increasing and isolating segments of the population from the wider opportunities offered by American society.

Behind these demands for cultural diversity is often a desire to destroy American society and the traditional values of Western civilization that it represents. There are two general motives. One is the belief that Western civilization is doomed. *Inc.* magazine editor Joel Kotlin and consultant Yoriko Kishimoto have argued that "it is time we Americans finally declare our independence from Europe and end our two-century-old fixation with western civilization." They see the 21st century as being "shaped by nations of Asia and the Third World." The U.S. should "transform the racial and historical identity of the country" to match this brave new world.[2]

The other motive is rooted in a left-wing ideology that sees the superiority of the West as evil. It is manifested in movements like that at Stanford University which succeeded in its protest against the teaching of a core course in Western civilization. These radicals equate wealth and power with immorality. They embrace alien cultures on the grounds that, since these cultures lost in competition with the West, they must be morally superior, failure being a sign of virtue.

Both schools are preaching dangerous nonsense. Historian J. N. Roberts, Warden to Merton College at Oxford University, has written:

> Almost all the master principles and ideas now reshaping the modern world emanate from the West; they have spread round the globe and other civilizations have crumbled before them. . . . "Modern" history can be defined as the approach march to the age dominated by the West.[3]

This age, spanning the last 500 years, generated the incredible progress that has broken the stagnation of previous centuries and, in some parts of the world, previous millennia. The secret of Western success, according to Roberts, is that "Europeans did not succumb to what they found but sought to master it":

> It is at least clear that an explanation of European inquisitiveness and adventurousness must lie deeper than economics, important though they may have been. It was not just greed which made Europeans feel that they could go out and take the world . . . . The idea of dominating nature was already about in their culture, waiting to be put to use.[4]

No one needs to apologize for a civilization whose hallmark has been a constant drive to push back the frontiers of human achievement. There is little to gain and very much to lose should the United States trade its Western heritage for that of any other culture.

Immigrants want to come to America because they desire to share in the fruits of the Western tradition. It would be suicidal to destroy that tradition. If today the United States seems to be losing in the competition with Asian rivals, it is because we have forgotten how to play the game our forefathers invented. The solution is not to abandon our Western heritage, but to recover it, to renew the spirit of "inquisitiveness and adventurousness" that made America great, to once again exhibit the confidence needed to master the challenges that face us rather than succumb to them.

The Need to Limit Immigration

The flood of immigrants is simply too much at once. The United States cannot be a safety valve for Mexico, the Caribbean, Asia and the entire Third World. The standard of life in the United States is far above what is experienced by the vast majority of the world's population. If the only real limit on the number of immigrants is how many want to come here, then there is no limit at all. The flow of immigrants from the Third World is unfair to those persons living across the Atlantic who want to establish themselves in the United States. These would-be immigrants from the European continent and the British Isles have the closest cultural ties with America but are restricted to a trickle under the law, compared to the legal and illegal influx of immigrants from Latin America and Asia. Our immigration policy needs to be revised to provide a proper balance. Not only must steps be taken to halt illegal immigration, but legal immigration should encourage newcomers from the areas most compatible with the United States.

America can benefit from immigration in the future as it has in the past. However, policymakers and opinion leaders need to be reminded that the United States is a sovereign nation with every right and duty to control its borders. Whenever people cross the border to enter the country they do so only with the permission of American authorities. Permission to do that depends on one simple principle: immigrants are not allowed to come to America whenever it is in their interest to do so, but only when it is in America's interest that they do so. The aim is not for aliens to come to the United States to improve themselves but to come here to improve the United States. That means that a rational immigration policy requires screening and careful selection as well as limits based on how many newcomers American society can absorb in a given time period.

In U.S. policy the interests of American citizens should prevail over the interests of others. It has taken three centuries to build out of a continental wilderness the wealthy and powerful nation that is now the United States. The benefits of that achievement rightly belong first and foremost to those who accomplished it and to their descendants. An unlimited flood of immigrants that would undermine the foundations of American society is simply not fair to American citizens. The first to be affected will be the most vulnerable members of society. The United States already has an urban underclass that needs uplifting. If public resources are to be used for health, education and welfare, citizens should have the first claim on these resources. The United States does not need to import poverty from around the world.

To be sure, it is hard for Americans to accept a policy of markedly-restricted immigration. We are a nation of immigrants, as the saying goes. But the end of the 20th century is a very different time from the 19th century. In an earlier era, the country was underpopulated, a nation of open lands. It could benefit from an open immigration policy. Today, the American frontier is closed. The country is an urban society. Its economy is no longer based on labor-intensive agriculture and unskilled factory hands. Newcomers cannot live on the land even if they wanted to. They expect jobs and a high degree of public services, the same services received by citizens. The cost of absorbing newcomers on such a large scale is beyond the means of an American society which has so many other demands on its resources. The United States cannot continue to operate as if conditions in 1988 were the same as in 1888 or 1788. Hundreds of millions of people around the world hunger for the freedom and material abundance that exists in America. But immigration cannot be the answer to their dreams. They must build their future in their own lands.

Chapter XI

Resurgence or Decline: America in the 1990s

The proper goal of public policy in the United States is the preservation of the liberties and the well-being of the American people in every respect, from economic to moral matters. National strength and national character are interrelated. The American experiment has survived for more than two centuries because of the sturdy, resilient character, common sense, enlightened self-interest and courage of the American people.

There are many strands in the fabric of American national strength. Economic security is certainly one of the principal strands. A slowing in the pace of prosperity, a decline in the wealth of the nation, or a fall in living standards would test the republican form of government. It would discourage the American people and encourage experimentation with extreme political ideas and economic systems. We know this from examining the history of the 1930s. Severe economic problems exacerbate social tensions and stimulate internal conflict. They also reduce the ability of the country to deal with threats beyond its borders.

That is not to say that it is necessary for a country to regard rapid economic growth as the ultimate objective of government. But growth must take place at a sufficient pace so that an expanding population is confronted with opportunities, not restrictions. And, of course, growth has to be sufficient to maintain the nation's place in the wider world. When nations have fallen in the past, it has not usually been because their capabilities declined in the absolute sense, but because they declined in a relative sense. Threats and rivals grew in power faster than they did until the balance shifted to the point where they could no longer cope with their problems.

The American people certainly want their economy to work in such a way that they are not placed in a position of subordination to other countries. In recent years, there has been an unfortunate school of thought that holds that the United States must accept a diminished global role and relinquish control over its own destiny. Americans need to be very wary of this view, for they surely do not want the country to drift into second-class status. One way that this can happen is by losing a measure of economic sovereignty, by losing the edge the United States gained during the first two-thirds of the 20th century.

Americans have before them the unhappy example of Great Britain, which had enormous power and wealth in the last century and the first part of this century. It was once called "the workshop of the world," with London as the center of world banking and the capital of a global empire. Now England finds itself in the bottom half of European states in living standards, a small island with only a fraction of its former military security. Because of economic erosion, Britain lacks the degree of freedom of action that it had before the world wars. Thoughtful Britons fear that political and economic change under a future Labor government could result in Britain becoming the equivalent of an East Bloc state, drab and deprived of its traditional liberties.

Yale historian Paul M. Kennedy has spent his life chronicling the decline of his native England. In his best-selling book, *The Rise and Fall of the Great Powers*, he states that England's "decline could intensify if a change in government led to large increases in social spending (rather than productive investment), higher taxation levels, a drop in business confidence and a flight from sterling."[1]

Such a dramatic shift is not inevitable nor is it ordained by forces that are beyond America's control. The United States holds an inherently stronger position than did England a century ago. America is a single continental nation-state; England's domain was scattered both geographically and culturally around the globe. London was the center of an empire, but an empire that was never successfully united into a self-sustaining economic system. In 1900, the British Isles still conducted almost half of its trade outside the Empire. And, in 1913, the United States sold more steel, finished and semifinished, to the open British colonies and dominions than did England, whereas British steel mills sold virtually nothing to the vast but protected American market. London held to the "free trade" sophistry long after her rivals had provided ample evidence of its failure.

Paul Kennedy has been rightly criticized for his pessimism. He has advised Americans to do as the English did, to simply decline gracefully rather than strive for a resurgence of strength and future greatness. But as the advertisements of one investment house proclaim, Americans don't just want to survive, they want to succeed. It is still within the power of the United States to turn things around.

The American people must be very careful to ensure that sound public policies are in effect, policies that renew and expand the nation's strength. We can learn from both the successes and the failures of those who have gone before us. Pursuing our own interests does not necessitate hostility to other nations or a blind adherence to the precise international commitments of today. Flexibility is as important for nations as for individuals. But the country cannot afford to yield in its determination to be Number One. It must not become subservient economically, militarily or in any other way to ambitious, aggressive states elsewhere in the world.

A determination to remain Number One entails assertiveness in many areas, including economics. It entails protection of the nation's land, labor, and capital, and their constructive use in building an independent future. It means that the brainpower and energies of the United States must be fully mobilized and that national strength must not be wasted in excessive welfare programs at home or abroad. The only true way to increase living standards is by growth. Progress by redistribution is only a mirage. Being Number One means being realistic about and vigilant towards the goals and the objectives of adversarial societies. It means that the country must uphold its moral traditions and make sure that its values are defended and advanced in its institutions of learning.

The United States already has paid a heavy toll for the mistaken views and policies it has indulged in during the past quarter century. The false "liberation" of the 1960s, what was once called "the greening of America," introduced deep divisions in society. It sapped the spirit that had built the country. It implanted the hurtful notion that complete tolerance is the ultimate value of a democracy and rootless individualism is the highest aspiration. Thus was born the "me" generation that wanted unlimited rights while rejecting all corresponding duties. For many years to come the United States will have to suffer the manifestations of this false "liberation:" the existence of groups that are hedonistic or nihilistic in outlook, the vestiges of the 1960s counterculture that was so hostile to American traditions and loyalties.

The United States also suffers economically from a liberal view of the world that easily accepts the idea of reduced American strength by making light of any and all threats to U.S. interests. This has eroded the American will to win in the global economic arena just as it earlier eroded America's will to safeguard its military security.

Today we need to strengthen our traditional patriotism and generate a new and expanded patriotism that, in the words of Kevin Phillips, causes Americans to feel very strongly about "defending Silicon Valley, the beach at Waikiki and U.S. neighborhoods threatened by drug trafficking." Phillips said that in this new patriotic mood the American people are "beginning to rethink U.S. vulnerability and remedies needed in economic rather than military terms."

This is the approach embodied in this set of goals for the 1990s. The overall recommendations are based on a rethinking of national needs. The program includes economic patriotism and a strategic trade and industrial policy that could be called an economic containment policy. More than 40 years ago, U.S. policy-makers defined the national interest in terms of a military containment policy. This military emphasis was necessary then and it continues to be necessary today. But the military containment policy has to be supplemented and expanded by a matching economic containment policy. The nature of the threat to America's well-being has changed and shifted in overall focus. All domestic, foreign and defense policies, from dealing with the trade deficit to immigration control to limits on wasteful federal spending, have to be considered parts of the national containment policy that safeguards vital American interests. As every high official in Washington swears upon taking his position, every American must pledge to defend his country "against all enemies, foreign and domestic."

Notes

CHAPTER I

1. Walt W. Rostow, quoted in *Business Month*, January, 1988, p. 47.
2. Roy Hofheinz and Kent Calder, *The Eastasia Edge* (New York: Basic Books, 1982), p. 46.
3. Dr. Donald Rousslang, *U.S. Trade-Related Employment: 1978-82* (U.S. International Trade Commission, Publication Number 1445, Washington, D.C., October, 1983), p. 66.
4. James C. Abegglen and Thomas A. Hout, "Facing Up to the Trade Gap with Japan." *Foreign Affairs*, Vol. 57, Fall, 1978, p. 148.
5. Barry Bluestone, *The Great American Job Machine: The Proliferation of Low-Wage Employment in the U.S. Economy* (Joint Economic Committee of the U.S. Congress, Washington, D.C.: U.S. Government Printing Office, 1986).
6. "The False Paradise of a Service Economy." *Business Week*, March 3, 1986, pp. 79-80.
7. *Ibid*, p. 80.
8. "Productivity 1960-1986: An International Comparison," *Economic Road Maps* (The Conference Board, Maps 2009-2010, Washington, D.C., April, 1987), p. 1.
9. Peter O. Peterson, "The Morning After." *The Atlantic*, 260 (October, 1987), p. 58.
10. Jared Taylor, *Shadows of the Rising Sun* (New York: William Morrow Co., 1983), pp. 53-54.

CHAPTER II

1. Chalmers Johnson, *MITI and the Japanese Miracle: The Growth of Industrial Policy 1925-1975* (Stanford: Stanford University Press, 1982), p. 19.
2. John Maynard Keynes, *General Theory of Employment, Interest and Money* (New York: Harcourt Brace & Co., 1936), p. 333.
3. Ludwig von Mises, *Omnipotent Government* (reprint of 1944 edition, Spring Mills: Libertarian Press, 1985), p. 92.
4. Friedrich List, *The National System of Political Economy* (reprint of 1846 edition, Fairfield: Augustus M. Kelley, 1977), p. 181.
5. Charles Wilson, "Treasure and Trade Balances: The Mercantilist Problem," in Charles Wilson, *Economic History and the Historian* (London: Weidenfeld & Nicolson, 1969), p. 61. See also Robert Gilpin, "Economic Interdependence and National Security in Historical Perspective," in Klaus Knorr and Frank N. Trager, eds., *Economic Issues and National Security* (Lawrence: Regents Press of Kansas, 1977).
6. Alexander Hamilton, "The Continentalist V," April 18, 1782, in Morton J. Frisch, ed., *Selected Writings and Speeches of Alexander Hamilton* (Washington, D.C.: American Enterprise Institute, 1985), p. 55.
7. John A. Kasson in Tom E. Terrill, *The Tariff Politics and American Foreign Policy 1874-1901* (Westport: Greenwood Press, 1973), p. 55.

8. Theodore Roosevelt, President, Address at the University of Minnesota, Minneapolis (Minn., April 4, 1903), in Hermann Hagedorn, ed., *The Works of Theodore Roosevelt* (Vol. XIII, New York: Collier & Son, 1926), p. 295.
9. George Shultz, U.S. Secretary of State, Address at Massachusetts Institute of Technology, Cambridge (Mass., April 28, 1982), in *Current Policy* (U.S. Department of State, Number 1070, Washington, D.C.: U.S. Government Printing Office), pp. 2-3.
10. George Gilder, Address at Manhattan Institute Seminar, New York (N.Y., July 13, 1987).
11. Charles P. Doran, "War and Power Dynamics: Economic Underpinnings." *International Studies Quarterly*, Vol. 27, December, 1983, p. 432.
12. Charles H. Ferguson, "From the People Who Brought You Voodoo Economics." *Harvard Business Review*, May-June, 1988, pp. 56-62.
13. Arnold Kramish, "The Bodaibo Syndrome: Maintaining Technological Leadership." *Global Affairs* (Summer, 1988), p. 102.
14. Paul W. Kuznits, "An East Asian Model of Economic Development: Japan, Taiwan and South Korea." *Economic Development and Cultural Change*, 36 (April, 1988).
15. Colby H. Chandler, Transcript of Manufacturing Press Conference, Washington, D.C., April 21, 1988, p. 1.

CHAPTER III

1. *Business Week*, February 1, 1988, p. 100.
2. C. Fred Bergsten, "Economic Imbalances and World Politics." *Foreign Affairs*, Vol. 65, Spring, 1987, p. 776.
3. Lawrence C. Fox, "The Dollar and the U.S. Economic Position: A Longer Range Perspective," in *Profiting from International Trade and Investment* (The Conference Board, Research Bulletin No. 221, Washington, D.C., June, 1988).
4. Caspar Weinberger, U.S. Secretary of Defense, *Annual Report to Congress: Fiscal Year 1987* (U.S. Department of Defense, Washington, D.C.: U.S. Government Printing Office, 1987), p. 63.
5. An original source for this statement cannot be found. However, U. Alexis Johnson confirmed, in a December 2, 1988, letter to USIC Educational Foundation, that it is generally consistent with what he often said in the scores of meetings with press and other media throughout Japan while he was U.S. ambassador there from 1966 to 1969.

CHAPTER IV

1. H. Ross Perot, quoted in *The Washington Post*, October 25, 1987, sec. C, p. 2.
2. William E. Simon, "Economic Priorities for the Next President." *Policy Review*, 44 (Summer, 1988), p. 20.
3. Hiroshi Kato, quoted in "Insular Culture's Global Ambition," *Insight*, July 18, 1988, p. 10.
4. Yasuhiro Nakasone, quoted in "Insular Culture's Global Ambition," *Insight*, July 18, 1988, p. 10.
5. *Industry Week*, February 1, 1988, p. 28.
6. George Gilder, "The Planetary Utility." *Policy Review*, 44 (Summer, 1988), pp. 50-53.
7. *Forbes*, 141 (February 22, 1988), p. 63.
8. John Bryant, U.S. Representative from Texas, 5th District, "Foreign Ownership in America," letter to district constituents, December, 1987.

NOTES

9. Pat Choate, quoted in *The Washington Post*, June 19, 1988, sec. C, p. 1.
10. Alfred A. Malabre, Jr., "U.S. Economy Grows Ever More Vulnerable To Foreign Influences." *The Wall Street Journal*, October 27, 1986, p. 1, col. 6.
11. Richard Drobnik, quoted in "U.S. Consultant: Financial Power Shifting to Japan," *The Washington Post*, May 17, 1988, sec. C, p. 6.
12. Charles H. Ferguson, "From the People Who Brought You Voodoo Economics." *Harvard Business Review*, 66 (May-June, 1988), p. 55.
13. Walter Olson, quoted in *Associate Memo* (The Manhattan Foundation, Number 11, New York, May 1, 1988), p. 4.
14. *The Economist*, October 17, 1987, p. 19.
15. Frank Gibney, *Japan: The Fragile Superpower* (revised edition, New York: New American Library, 1980).
16. Peter F. Drucker, quoted in *The Wall Street Journal*, May 26, 1987, p. 32.
17. *Ibid*.

CHAPTER V

1. Robert H. Ballance and Stuart Sinclair, *Collapse and Survival: Industry Strategies in a Changing World* (London: George Allen & Unwin, 1983), p. 14.
2. *Ibid*, p. 8.
3. Kevin P. Phillips, *Staying on Top: The Business Case for a National Industrial Strategy* (New York: Random House, 1984), p. 9.
4. Chalmers Johnson, *The Industrial Policy Debate* (San Francisco: Institute for Contemporary Studies Press, 1984), p. 11.
5. Pierre du Pont, "Kamikaze Economics." *Policy Review*, 33 (Fall 1985), p. 43.
6. John Maynard Keynes, "Mitigation by Tariff," in *Essays in Persuasion* (reprint of 1931 edition, New York: W. W. Norton, 1963), p. 274.
7. *Ibid*, p. 277.
8. Frank Taussig, *The Tariff History of the United States* (reprint of 1931 edition, New York: Capricorn Books, 1964), p. 519.
9. Ronald A. Morse, "Japan's Drive for Pre-Eminence." *Foreign Policy*, Vol. 69, Winter, 1987-1988, p. 3.
10. George Gilder, Address at Manhattan Institute Seminar, New York (N.Y., July 13, 1987).
11. Christopher Wood, "A Depression in our Future?" *The American Spectator*, February, 1988, p. 18.
12. Morse, p. 8.
13. Robert T. Green and Trina L. Larsen, "Only Retaliation Will Open Up Japan." *Harvard Business Review*, November-December, 1987, p. 22.
14. William Niskanen, *Reaganomics* (New York: Oxford University Press, 1988), p. 137-38.
15. Deborah Allen, "The Declining Dollar: Limited Relief for the Few," in *The Domestic World Forecast* (Claremont Economics Institute, Claremont, California, February, 1987), pp. 17-24.
16. Robert Eisner, "Not So Good, Not So Bad." *The World & I*, July, 1988, p. 25.
17. Wolfgang F. Stopler, "After Oil Euphoria, Problems Will Remain," *The Washington Post*, March 25, 1986, sec. C, p. 4.
18. Daniel Burstein in *The New York Times*, April 28, 1985, sec. 4, p. 23, col. 2.
19. C. Fred Bergsten, *The Dilemmas of the Dollar* (New York: New York University Press, 1975), p. 25.
20. Alfred L. Malabre, Address to the Annual Meeting of the Committee for Monetary Research and Education, The Union Club, New York (N.Y., July 22, 1987).

CHAPTER VI

1. Thomas Jefferson, letter to Frederic Bastiat, in *Writings of Thomas Jefferson* (Vol. XIV, Washington, D.C.: Jefferson Memorial Foundation, 1903), p. 260.
2. Alton D. Stay, testimony before the U.S. House of Representatives Armed Services Committee (96th Congress, 2nd Session, Washington, D.C., November 13, 1980).
3. Corelli Barnett, *The Collapse of British Power* (New York: William Morrow & Co., 1972), p. 92.
4. *Civil Preparedness Review, Part 1: Emergency Preparedness and Industrial Mobilization* (Joint Committee on Defense Production of the U.S. Congress, 95th Congress, 1st Session, Washington, D.C.: U.S. Government Printing Office, 1977).
5. Caspar Weinberger, U.S. Secretary of Defense, *Annual Report to Congress: Fiscal Year 1985* (U.S. Department of Defense, Washington, D.C.: U.S. Government Printing Office, 1985), p. 93.
6. John N. Ellison, Jeffrey W. Frumkin and Timothy W. Stanley, eds., *Mobilizing U.S. Industry: A Vanishing Option for National Security?* (Boulder: Westview Press, 1988), pp. 104-105.
7. Robert Eisner, "Not So Good, Not So Bad." *The World & I*, July, 1988, p. 22-23.
8. Robert C. Fabrie, "Structural Change in the U.S. Industrial Base: Its Impact on National Defense," in Hardy L. Merritt and Luther F. Carter, eds., *Mobilization and National Defense* (Washington, D.C.: National Defense University Press, 1985), p. 100.
9. Adm. Charles A.H. Trost, quoted by L. Edgar Prina, "The Mathematics of Retrenchment." *Sea Power* (Navy League of the United States, Arlington, Virginia, March, 1987), p. 20.
10. George Shultz, U.S. Secretary of State, Address at Massachusetts Institute of Technology, Cambridge (Mass., April 28, 1982), in *Current Policy* (U.S. Department of State, Number 1070, Washington, D.C.: U.S. Government Printing Office). p. 1.
11. William P. Wadbrook in Robert L. Pfaltzgraff and Uri Ra'anan, eds., *The Defense Mobilization Infrastructure: Problems and Priorities* (Hamden: Archon Books, 1983), p. 26.
12. Stephen S. Cohen and John Zysman, *Manufacturing Matters: The Myth of the Post-Industrial Economy* (New York: Basic Books, 1987), p. 26.
13. Aron Katsenelinboigen, "Will Glasnost Bring the Reactionaries to Power?" *Orbis*, 32 (Spring, 1988), pp. 217-230.
14. *Ibid*, p. 227.

CHAPTER VII

1. A.P. Thirlwill, "Deindustrialization in the U.K." *Lloyd's Bank Review* (London, April, 1982), p. 24.
2. Julian Gresser, *Partners in Prosperity: Strategic Industries for the U.S. and Japan* (New York: McGraw-Hill, 1984), p. 46.
3. Stephen S. Cohen and John Zysman, *Manufacturing Matters: The Myth of the Post-Industrial Economy* (New York: Basic Books, 1987), p. xiii.
4. *Ibid*, p. 19.
5. *Ibid*, p. xiii.
6. *Ibid*, p. 95.
7. Robert W. Galvin, *Vital Speeches*, August 15, 1987, p. 649.
8. Charles H. Ferguson, Address to Manhattan Institute, New York (N.Y., July 13, 1987).

NOTES

9. Irving Kristol, quoted in *The Wall Street Journal*, May 13, 1988, p. 16.
10. Alfred D. Chandler, *The Visible Hand: The Managerial Revolution in American Business* (Cambridge: Harvard University Press, 1977), p. 315.
11. H. Ross Perot, quoted in *The Washington Post*, October 25, 1987, sec. C, p. 2.
12. Kristol, p. 16.
13. Neil Pierce, quoted in *The Philadelphia Enquirer*, September 14, 1987, sec. A, p. 13.
14. Chandler, p. 339.
15. Christopher Wood, "A Depression in our Future?" *The American Spectator*, February, 1988, p. 18.
16. Louis Lowenstein, quoted in *The New York Times*, May 11, 1988, sec. A, p. 27.
17. *Ibid.*
18. Perot, sec. C, p. 2.
19. *Ibid.*
20. Peter W. Huber, *The Legal Revolution and its Consequences* (New York: Basic Books, 1988), p. 10.
21. Mitch McConnell, U.S. Senator from Kentucky, "Sue for a Million" press conference, U.S. Capitol, Washington, D.C., June 7, 1988.
22. *Insuring Our Future: Report of the Governor's Advisory Commission on Liability Insurance* (Office of the Governor, Albany, New York, April 7, 1986), p. 9.

CHAPTER VIII

1. Charles T. Maxwell, energy analyst, in Kathryn M. Welling, "Crude Prospects: Charlie Maxwell on the Outlook for Oil." *Barron's*, May 9, 1988, p. 15.
2. William Safire, quoted in *The New York Times*, October 28, 1987, sec. A, p. 31.
3. William C. Mott, ed., *Strategic Minerals: A Resource Crisis* (Washington, D.C.: National Strategy Information Center, 1981), pp. 25-27.
4. John Ellison, *Evolution of U.S. Mobilization Policy*. Unpublished manuscript, Washington, D.C., June, 1987.
5. R. Scott Fosler in *Economic Review* (Federal Reserve Bank of Kansas City, Kansas City, Missouri, May, 1988), p. 15.
6. Rodger Swearingen, "The Soviet Far East, East Asia and the Pacific — Strategic Dimensions," in *Siberia and the Soviet Far East: Strategic Dimensions in Multinational Perspective* (Stanford: The Hoover Institution Press, 1987), p. 264.
7. *Ibid*, p. 265.
8. Joseph S. Nye, "Japan," in David D. Deese and Joseph S. Nye, eds., *Energy and Security* (Cambridge: Ballinger, 1981), p. 217.

CHAPTER IX

1. Chester E. Finn, Jr., "The Social Studies Debate." *The American Spectator*, 21 (May 1988), p. 36.
2. Albert Rees, *The Economics of Trade Unions* (Chicago: University of Chicago Press, 1967), p. 194.
3. Thomas Sowell, *Knowledge and Decisions* (New York: Basic Books, 1980), p. 173.
4. *Time*, June 20, 1988, p. 50.

CHAPTER X

1. *Estimated Costs of Illegal Immigration to U.S. Taxpayers* (Central Office, U.S. Immigration and Naturalization Service, Washington, D.C., Fall, 1983), in Donald L. Huddle, Arthur F. Corwin and Gordon J. MacDonald, *Illegal Immigration: Job Displacement and Social Cost* (American Immigration Control Foundation, Monterey, Virginia, 1985), p.10.
2. Joel Kotlin and Yoriko Kishimoto, "America's Asian Destiny," *The Washington Post*, July 3, 1988, sec. C, p. 1.
3. J. N. Roberts, *The Triumph of the West* (Boston: Little, Brown, 1985), p. 30.
4. *Ibid*, p. 118.

CHAPTER XI

1. Paul M. Kennedy, *The Rise and Fall of the Great Powers* (New York: Random House, 1987), p. 481.

Selected Bibliography

Ballance, Robert H., and Sinclair, Stuart. *Collapse and Survival: Industry Strategies in a Changing World.* London: George Allen & Unwin, 1983.

Barnett, Corelli. *The Collapse of British Power.* New York: William Morrow and Co., 1972.

_____. *The Price and the Fall.* New York: The Free Press, 1986.

Bergsten, C. Fred. *The Dilemmas of the Dollar.* New York: New York University Press, 1975.

Chandler, Alfred D. *The Visible Hand: The Managerial Revolution in American Business.* Cambridge: Harvard University Press, 1977.

Cipolla, Carlo M., ed. *The Economic Decline of Empires.* London: Methuen & Co., 1970.

Clark, Wilson, and Page, Jake. *Energy, Vulnerability and War: Alternatives for America.* New York: W. W. Norton, 1981.

Cohen, Stephen S., and Zysman, John. *Manufacturing Matters: The Myth of the Post-Industrial Economy.* New York: Basic Books, 1987.

Coleman, D. C., ed. *Revisions in Mercantilism.* London: Methuen & Co., 1969.

Desse, David D., and Nye, Joseph S., eds. *Energy and Security.* Cambridge: Ballinger Books, 1981.

Earle, Edward Mead, ed. *Makers of Modern Strategy.* Princeton: Princeton University Press, 1943.

Eckes, Alfred E., Jr. *The United States and the Global Struggle for Minerals.* Austin: University of Texas Press, 1979.

Ellison, John N., Frumkin, Jeffrey W., and Stanley, Timothy W., eds. *Mobilizing U.S. Industry: A Vanishing Option for National Security?* Boulder: Westview Press, 1988.

Frisch, Morton J., ed. *Selected Writings and Speeches of Alexander Hamilton.* Washington, D.C.: American Enterprise Institute, 1985.

Gibney, Frank. *Japan: The Fragile Superpower.* Revised edition. New York: New American Library, 1980.

Gresser, Julian. *Partners in Prosperity: Strategic Industries for the U.S. and Japan.* New York: McGraw-Hill, 1984.

Harrigan, Anthony, ed. *Putting America First: A Conservative Trade Alternative.* Washington, D.C.: U.S. Industrial Council Educational Foundation, 1987.

Hofheinz, Roy, and Calder, Kent. *The Eastasia Edge.* New York: Basic Books, 1982.

Johnson, Chalmers, ed. *The Industrial Policy Debate.* San Francisco: Institute for Contemporary Studies Press, 1984.

_____. *MITI and the Japanese Miracle: The Growth of Industrial Policy 1925-1975.* Stanford: Stanford University Press, 1982.

Kegley, Charles W., Jr., and Wittkopf, Eugene R. *The Global Agenda: Issues and Perspectives.* New York: Random House, 1984.

Kennedy, Paul M. *The Rise and Fall of the Great Powers.* New York: Random House, 1987.

Keynes, John Maynard. *The General Theory of Employment, Interest and Money.* New York: Harcourt Brace and Co., 1936.

_____. *Essays in Persuasion.* 1st Printing 1932. New York: W. W. Norton, 1963.
Knorr, Klaus. *The Power of Nations: The Political-Economy of International Relations.* New York: Basic Books, 1975.
Knorr, Klaus, and Trager, Frank N., eds. *Economic Issues and National Security.* Lawrence: Regents Press of Kansas, 1977.
List, Friedrich. *The National System of Political Economy.* 1st printing 1885. Fairfield: Augustus M. Kelley, 1977.
Margiotta, Frank, ed. *Evolving Strategic Realities: Implications for Policy-makers.* Washington, D.C.: National Defense University Press, 1980.
McCormick, Gordon H., and Bissell, Richard E., eds. *Strategic Dimensions of Economic Behavior.* New York: Praeger, 1984.
McCracken, Samuel. *The War Against the Atom.* New York, Basic Books, 1982.
Merrit, Hardy L., and Carter, Luther F., eds. *Mobilization and National Defense.* Washington, D.C.: National Defense University Press, 1985.
Modelski, George. *Long Cycles in World Politics.* Seattle: University of Washington Press, 1986.
Mott, William C., ed. *Strategic Minerals: A Resource Crisis.* Washington, D.C.: National Strategy Information Center, 1981.
Niskanen, William. *Reaganomics.* New York: Oxford University Press, 1988.
Pfaltzgraff, Robert L., and Ra'anan, Uri, eds. *The Defense Mobilization Infrastructure: Problems and Priorities.* Hamden: Archon Books, 1983.
Phillips, Kevin P. *Staying on Top: The Business Case for a National Industrial Strategy.* New York: Random House, 1984.
Rees, Albert. *The Economics of Trade Unions.* Chicago: University of Chicago Press, 1967.
Reynolds, Robert L. *Europe Emerges: Transition Toward an Industrial World-Wide Society 600-1750.* Madison: University of Wisconsin Press, 1967.
Roberts, J. N. *The Triumph of the West.* Boston: Little, Brown, 1985.
Schlossstein, Steven. *Trade Wars: Greed, Power and Industrial Policy on Opposite Sides of the Pacific.* New York: Congdon & Weed, 1984.
Silberner, Edmund. *The Problem of War in Nineteenth Century Economic Thought.* Princeton: Princeton University Press, 1946.
Smith, Adam. *The Wealth of Nations.* Reprint of 1937 Cannan ed. New York: The Modern Library, 1965.
Sowell, Thomas. *Knowledge and Decisions.* New York: Basic Books, 1980.
Swearingen, Robert, ed. *Siberia and the Soviet Far East.* Stanford: The Hoover Press, 1987.
Taussig, Frank. *The Tariff History of the United States.* 1st Printing 1931. New York: Capricorn Books, 1964.
Taylor, Jared. *Shadows of the Rising Sun.* New York: William Morrow Co., 1983.
Terrill, Tom E. *The Tariff, Politics and American Foreign Policy 1874-1901.* Westport: Greenwood Press, 1973.
Vawter, Roderick L. *Industrial Mobilization: The Relevant History.* Rev. ed. Washington, D.C.: National Defense University Press, 1983.
Wilson, Charles. *Economic History and the Historian.* London: Weidenfeld & Nicolson, 1969.

Subject Index

Acid rain, 101-103
American assets. *See* Real estate; U.S. assets
American companies. *See* Mergers; Takeovers; U.S. companies
American people, illusion of invincibility and, 2. *See also* United States
American values, decline of, 19
Anti-Americanism in Japan, 54
Anti-nuclearism, 98, 100-101
Antitrust laws
   archaic, 15-16
   exemption of labor unions from, 107
   need to change, 79
   restrictive, 47
Arab oil states, new industries replacing U.S. exports to, 18
Assets, sale to foreigners of American, 6. *See also* Capital
Automobiles, Japanese capacity in U.S. for manufacturing, 33

Balance of payments deficit (U.S.), 59
Balance of trade. *See* Trade balance
Banks
   competition in United States between American and Japanese, 38
   failures of, 84-85
   goals of Japanese, 39
   largest, 38
   role and control of, 35
Bilingual education, 117
"Black ship phenomenon," 2
Brazil, 8
Bretton Woods system, collapse of, 59
Business community, social issues and, 115-16
Business cycle, vulnerability of American firms to, 47

Business-government partnership successes, 44, 79

California, Japanese economic penetration of, 35
Canada
   acid rain and, 102-103
   French-speaking minority in, 117
   imported electric power from, 93
Capital
   economic growth dependent on, 75
   invested outside of U.S. by American firms, 40
   low level of formation by American firms and citizens, 33
   role of foreign, 38
   transfer to Third World of American, 18
Cartel-like relationships in Japan, 38
Chemical companies, foreign-owned (in United States), 36
China, Open Door policy in, 13. *See also* People's Republic of China; Taiwan
Clean Air Act, 102
Coal, 93-95
Cold War, 69
Community, emphasis on, 115-16
Competition with foreign companies, 40-42
Computer industry, U.S. dependent on Japan, 16
Conservatives, 43-44
Consumption-encouraging tax changes in U.S., 21-22
Credit purchases by Americans, 18
Crime, unions and organized, 107
Crisis, industrial base for mobilization in case of, 64-65
Critical raw materials, 15, 55, 57
Currency value as reflection of health of economy, 59. *See also* Dollar; Yen

Debt
  foreign financing of U.S. federal, 32
  Third World, 56
Defense
  industrial base for, 66
  of Japan, 25-27, 53
  sharing the burden of, 25-27
  spending for U.S., 22-23
  See also Military-industrial base of national power; Strategic industries
Deficits. *See* U.S. deficits
Depression, explanation for the Great, 48, 50-51, 85
Detente with USSR, 69
Developing countries, U.S. manufacturing and assembly work in, 41
Disclosure legislation, blocking of, 36
Dollar
  devaluation of, 7, 39, 45, 55-59
  inflation and devaluation of, 56, 57
  price of petroleum and value of, 58
  standard of living and fall in value of, 61
  tariffs and devaluation of, 57
Duties. *See* Tariffs

Eastasian economic growth, 2. *See also* Japan, other Asian nations
Economic dependency, dangers of, 14
Economic growth, 121-22
  dependent on capital accumulation, 75
  labor intensive, 4
  two forms of, 75
Economic mobilization, 65-68
Economic nationalism, 14-15
Economic planning
  conservatives and, 43-44
  as missing component in formulating national security policy, 63
  special interest groups and, 64
Economic sovereignty, loss of U.S., 32
Economic strength
  as key to national wealth and power, 11, 121
  military strength and, 63
Electric power, 98-101
  imported from Canada, 93
Employment
  decline in industrial jobs in advanced capitalistic economies, 75
  movement away from industrial, 4
  See also Jobs; Labor
Energy
  coal, 93-95
  electric, 93, 98-101
  Japanese and U.S. use of, *100*
  petroleum, 6-7, 14, 18, 58, 91, 92, 100
Energy independence for United States, 91-93, 100
Entitlement benefits, 6, 112
Environment
  absence of Mexican protection of, 94
  acid rain and, 101-103
Exports, 45
  half price of U.S., 56
  trade deficit and increased, 47, 70
  to USSR, 70-71

Fair trade, 9. *See also* Free trade
Families, quality of life and second incomes and, 4
Federal spending as percent of GNP, 6
Financial institutions. *See* Banks; Lending institutions
Financial markets, electronic integration of, 53. *See also* Markets
Financial power, shift to Japan, 38
Ford-McCumber act, 50
Foreign aid
  by Japan, 29
  by United States, 18, 27-29, 59
  by USSR, 29
Foreign companies
  control of American subsidiaries of, 35
  profits used to purchase American assets, 4-5
  subsidization of, 47
Foreign debt of United States, 6
Foreign financial power in the United States, 38-40
Foreign investment by United States, capital outflows for, 59
Foreign investment in the United States
  committee on, 36
  oversight of, 37
Foreign investors, tax exemptions for, 32
Foreign ownership of American assets
  getting facts about, 34
  resistance to disclosure of, 33, 36
Foreign policy, trade policy as an arm of, 13, 73-74

SUBJECT INDEX

Foreign-produced components of military or aerospace significance, 66-68
Foreign trade deficit. *See* trade deficit of the United States
Foreign trade strategies, 47-48
Free trade, 8, 11, 46
  American policy based on, 9
  dependent and vulnerability from, 15
  v. mercantilism, 11-12
  theory of comparative advantage and, 75-76

Global economy, 5, 51-53
Globalism, lobbyists and, 4-5
GNP. *See* Gross National Product
Gold standard, 59
Goods produced abroad in U.S.-owned plants, 40
Government, role in economy, 43-45, 64
Grace Commission, 24
Greater East Asian Co-Prosperity Sphere, 7
Great Britain, 122
Gross National Product (GNP)
  trade deficit as subtraction from, 46
  from value-added manufacturing, 76

Hawaii, Japanese economic invasion of, 35

Immigration and immigrants into United States, 116-17, 119-20
Imports
  advantage of restricting selected, 57
  fee on oil, 93
  U.S. trade deficit and flood of manufactured, 13
  U.S. trade deficit and reduction in, 47, 70
Income, median (U.S. males), 4
Industrial base
  for military power, 66-68
  for mobilization in case of war, crisis, or trade disruption, 64
  required to be a Great Power, 10, 64-65
  See also Strategic industries
Industrial employment, movement away from, 4. *See also* Jobs
Industrial policy, 76
  foreign, 56

Industrial-technological leadership, America's loss of, 16, 46
Inflation
  devaluation and, 56, 57
  trade deficit and, 46
Infrastructure, investment in U.S., 6
Innovation
  control of results of, 77
  economic growth from, 75
  See also Technology
Insurance, 86-87
  saving and loan institutions and, 85
Interagency National Acid Precipitation Program (INAPP), 102
Interest rate, flow of foreign investment funds into United States and, 60
International v. global economy, 51-53
Internationalism, 13
International trade
  American tradition and, 12-14
  foreign policy and national security and, 74
  since World War II, 12
Investment
  in American productive capacity, 18
  insurance companies as source of funds for, 86
  net rate of U.S., 6
  tax cuts failure to stimulate, 21
  U.S. balance of payments and flow of funds for, 60

Japan
  American technological decline and, 16
  anti-Americanism in, 54
  automobile manufacturing in U.S., 33
  cartel-like relationships in, 38
  cost of defense of, 25-27
  as a fragile superpower, 39-40
  fusion of economic and national drives in, 2
  government administrative guidance for business in, 17
  joint government-private endeavors to strengthen firms against foreign rivals, 79
  MITI in, 4, 79
  national goals of, 53-54, 79
  overseas investment and control, 7-8
  Perry's opening of, 2

plan-rational v. market-rational state, 9
racial attitudes in, 34
role of trading companies in, 14
savings in, 7
U.S. defense of, 25-27, 53
U.S. leverage over, 40
Japanese banks and financial institutions, 35
goals of, 39
in the United States, 38
Japanese executives and managers, 3
in America, 34
Japanese firms, maintenance of market share by profit adjustments, 60-61
Japanese lobbying and public relations in U.S., 7, 33, 37
"Japanese model," reasons for success of, 14
Japanese technology and products, American dependence on, 34-35
Jobs
best-paying and most productive, 3-4
creating, 49
declining numbers of industrial, 75
good industrial traded for poor service, 4, 46
lost American, 3, 42
low-paying in United States, 3, 4
movement overseas of American, 42
number of new, 4
Joint Economic Committee, 3

Labor
mandated benefits and, 112-13
unionized portion of, 105
Labor law, reform of, 108-109
Labor unions
antitrust exemption of, 107
economy and, 105-108
middle class and family issues and, 111
public employees, 105-107, 108
public reaction to abuses by, 109
radical fringe of, 111
Latin America
dollars from, 36
as net exporter to United States, 8
Lending institutions, 84-87. *See also* Banks
Liberalism, utopian goal of, 11
Loans, Third World bad, 18
Lobbying, Japanese, 7, 33, 37

Lobbyists and globalism, 4-5

"Made in USA" label, erroneous, 40
Manufacturing
division of world, 43
growth-inducing characteristics of, 75
industrial chains linking service sector to, 76-77
research and development tied to, 77
Market extension operations, 40
Markets
limited overseas, 56
management and, 83
orderly, 83-84
Mercantilism, 11-12
benefits of, 14
lowering profits to maintain market share, 60-61
Mergers, 81
Military bases
foreign aid in exchange for, 24
as pork barrel projects, 23-24
Military-industrial base of national power, 63-65. *See also* Strategic industries
Military pensions and benefits, 24-25
Military strength
economic strength and, 63
industrial capacity and technological innovation and, 68
science and industry and, 74
Minerals, 93-95, 101
Minimum wage, 110
Ministry of International Trade and Industry (MITI) in Japan, 4, 79
Model, static economic, 75
Money and power, 59-61

National Defense Stockpile (U.S.), 94
National Labor Relations Board, 109
National security policy
advanced industrial technologies and, 68
foreign policy and international trade and, 73-74
lack of economic planning in formulating, 63
Nationalism, 2
v. global community, 106
NATO, 25-26
Nuclear reactors for electric power, 98-101

Offshore production, two kinds of, 40-41
Oil. See Petroleum
Oil embargo, threat of crippling, 92
OPEC, price hike and embargo of 1979, 14, 18, 91
Open Door policy in China, 13, 46
Overseas markets limited by foreign industrial policies and Third World debt, 56
Overseas subsidiaries of U.S. companies, 40

Panic, possibility of global, 53. See also Crisis; War
Pension plans, private, 87-89
Pensions, military and federal, 25
People's Republic of China, 8, 93
Petroleum
  cost of industrial production and price of, 58
  foreign interest in American production facilities for, 92
  imports into United States, 6-7, 91
  prices of, 13, 14, 58, 91
  See also Energy independence for United States; Oil embargo; OPEC
Petroleum industry, steps to revive domestic, 92-93
Philippines, blackmail of United States by, 24
Policy
  decisions on public, 43-44
  industrial, 44-45, 77
  management of U.S. economic, 38, 77
  special interest groups' undermining of ability to make national, 64
  technological decline resulting from U.S., 16
  trade and foreign, 13
  U.S. tax, 21-22, 32
  U.S. trade deficit and, 45
Political action committees, foreign-funded, 37
Political economy, two systems of, 9
Population and facilities, excessive concentration of, 97
Production
  for American market, 42
  raw materials needed for high technology, 15
  See also Manufacturing; Offshore production

Productivity
  economic growth from, 75
  of labor force in United States, 4
  lower growth of, 6
  pensions and improved, 87
Profits
  importance of, 49
  mercantilist states maintaining market share by temporarily lowering margins of (Japan), 60-61
  repatriated by American companies from overseas production, 40
Protectionism, 12, 13, 48
  dollar devaluation and, 57
Protectionist barriers, U.S.-owned foreign factories and foreign, 40
Public policy decisions, 43-44, 123

Quotas, sustained bilateral trade deficits and country-specific, 54

Racketeer-Influence Corrupt Organization (RICO) Act, 107
Railroads, 108-109
Raw materials
  critical, 15, 55, 57
  needed for high technology production, 15
Reagan administration
  lack of control over imports and over collapse of the dollar, 56
  market reforms and, 83
  policies of, 22, 55
  priorities of, 61
  supply side economics and, 21-22
Real estate, foreign ownership of American, 34
Recession, devaluation to deal with trade deficit and, 61
Refugees, 117. See also Immigration and immigrants into the United States
Regional development in United States, 97
Republican party, tariffs and, 12
Research
  anti-trust laws limiting American, 15-16
  decentralizing government facilities for, 96
Research and development programs
  national security and, 68

too expensive without an industrial
    base, 77
Retaliation, country-specific, 54-55
Retirement plans, 88. *See also* Pensions
Right-to-work laws, 109
Russia. *See* USSR
Rust belt, 3

Savings
    fall in rate of U.S., 19
    pensions as, 87
    See also Thrift
Savings and loan institutions, cost of
    merging or bailing out, 85
Scientifc attaches, 16
Semiconductors, Japanese producers of, 16
Service economy, 4
    critical industries in, 77-79
    industrial chains linking manufacturing
        to, 76-77
    national strategy needed for, 78
Sherman Act, 107
Smoot-Hawley, 48-51
Social Security, 88-89
South Africa, 94
South Korea
    economic offensive of, 3, 8
    strategies to advance export-oriented
        industrial system, 16-17
Soviets. *See* USSR
Spanish language in United States, 117
Special interest groups, national economic
    policy undermined by, 64
Standard of living, fall in American, 61
State(s)
    resource-based U.S. regions and, 93-98
    significance and nature of "size" of, 11
Steel industries, Japanese and Korean, 16
Strategic industries, 75-77
    definition of, 65-66
    imports and, 66
    need for protection for, 58
    trade balances in, 66
Strategic minerals, 94-95. *See also*
    Minerals
Strategic Petroleum Reserve, 95
Supply-side economics, failure of, 21-22
Sustained bilateral trade deficits, U.S.
    quotas and, 54

Taiwan, 8
    strategies to advance export-oriented
        industrial system in, 16-17
Takeovers and business organization,
    79-83
Tariffs
    country-specific, 54
    dollar devaluation and, 57
    protective, 12, 49-50
Tax cuts, influence on consumption, 21
Tax exemptions
    for foreign investors, 32
    on pension income, 88-89
Tax reform, 21-22
Tax revenues, increase in U.S., 22
Technology
    dependence of U.S. on Japanese, 34-35
    foreign use of, 15, 78
    military power and, 68
    transfer from U.S. of new, 15, 97
    U.S. as importer of, 16, 78
    U.S. policy causing decline of, 16
    See also Innovation
Third World
    loss of U.S. competitive capability to
        export to, 3
    results of transfer of U.S. capital to, 18
    U.S. lending to, 18, 28
    See also Developing countries
Thorium, 101
Thrift, 18
Tort reform, 86-87
Trade
    industrial base for mobilization in case of
        disruption of, 64
    unions power to interfere with, 107
    See also Free trade; International trade;
        Mercantilism
Trade balance
    free trade, mercantilism, and a favorable,
        10
Trade deficit of United States, 3, 6,
    45, 59-60
    boosting exports and curtailing imports
        and, 70
    import restrictions v. devaluation to
        deal with, 61
    Japanese portion of, 51
    oil imports and, 91
    since 1982, 13
    sustained bilateral, 54
    tariffs as part of solution to, 49-50

SUBJECT INDEX

Trade policy
  basic point for reform of U.S., 46-67
  foreign policy and, 13
Trade problems, need to deal on a country-specific basis with, 54-55
Trade surpluses of United States, 13, 59
Trade war, 9, 47
Transnationalism, 41
Trucking industry, 109

Underdeveloped countries. *See* Developing countries; Third World
Unemployable underclass, 110
Unemployment, 3
  new benefits to employees and, 113
  See also Jobs
Unions. *See* Labor unions
United States
  competitive status of, 3
  danger of deficits of, 19-20
  declining share of world GNP, 17
  economic sovereignty of, 122
  foreign financial power in, 38-40
  foreign imports into, 3
  global role of, 122
  leverage over Japan, 40
  loss of surplus wealth of, 5
  lost lead in critical industries, 3
  market-rational v. plan-rational state, 9
  productive industry needed in, 15
  slowing investment in productive capacity of, 18
  technological decline of, 16, 17
  traditional American trade policies and, 12-14
  vulnerability of, 67
U.S. assets
  bargain prices of, 57
  foreign-held dollars to buy, 33
  Japanese purchase of, 7
  purchased by foreign firms, 4-5, 7
  resistance to disclosure of foreign ownership of, 33
U.S. companies
  financial community and, 82
  as mere distributors of Japanese products, 16
  overseas subsidiaries of, 40
  profits repatriated from overseas sales of overseas production of, 40

U.S. defense
  budget and expenses for, 22-27
  of Japan, 25-27
U.S. deficits
  defense and, 22-23
  strategy to reduce, 22
  supply-side economics and, 21
  twin trade and budget, 19-20, 32
U.S. dependence on Japanese goods and technology, 34-35
U.S. economic foundation, weakness of, 6-7
U.S. economic policies, management of, 38
U.S. economy, de-Americanization of, 38
U.S. foreign aid, 27-29
U.S. government officials, foreign groups employment of former, 37
U.S. National Defense Stockpile of strategic minerals, 94
U.S. policy, technological decline from, 16
USSR
  danger to United States and, 72-73
  desirable and undesirable U.S. trade with, 73
  global strategy of, 28-29
  military equipment production of, 71
  military forces of, 26
  nationalism of, 72
  nuclear reactors for electric power, 100
  as U.S. source of strategic minerals, 94
  street gangs in, 72
  trade with, 68-73
U.S. tax policies, 21-22, 32

Veterans. *See* Military pensions and benefits
Vietnam War, 19, 59

Wages, 110
War, industrial base for mobilization in case of, 64-65
Welfare costs, 110
Western civilization, 118-19
West Germany, trade with U.S., 53
Women in workforce, 4
World Bank, 28
World economy
  internationalism and, 13
  OPEC price hike and, 14

Yen, bargain in U.S. for Japanese companies operating with, 60

Name Index

Abegglen, James C., on industries affected by America's loss of competitive capability, 3

Ballance, Robert H., on trade and industrial policies, 43
Banks, James A., on global community, 106
Barnett, Corelli, on industries needing protection, 65
Bentsen, Sen. Lloyd, 37
Bergsten, C. Fred
  on operations of mercantilist countries, 60
  on supply-side economics, 21
Bryant, Rep. John, on blocking of disclosure legislation, 36
Burstein, Daniel, on bargains in United States for Japanese companies, 60

Calder, Kent, on Eastasian nationalism, 2
Chandler, Alfred D., on how firms that grow by merger achieve success, 81, 83
Chandler, Colby H., on decline of manufacturing in America, 17
Choate, Pat, on Japanese lobbying in Washington, 37
Cohen, Stephen S.
  on global struggle for manufacturing technology, 76-77
  on military power depending on industrial capacity and technological innovation, 68

Doran, Charles P., on benefits of mercantilism, 14

Drobnik, Richard, on shift to Japan of world financial power, 38
Drucker, Peter F., on capital invested outside of United States by American firms, 40, 41
du Pont, Pete, on Smoot-Hawley, 48

Earle, Edward Mead, on interrelationship of factors in national power and political economy, 63
Eckes, Alfred E., on U.S. jobs lost due to trade deficit, 3
Eisner, Robert, on devaluation and protectionism, 57
Ellison, John, on Munitions Board and National Security Resources Board, 96

Fabrie, Robert C., on reliability of offshore suppliers, 67
Ferguson, Charles H., on loss of America's industrial-technological leadership, 16, 80
Finn, Chester E., Jr., on social studies in schools, 106
Fosler, R. Scott, on regional U.S. development, 97
Fox, Lawrence A., on U.S. tax and national expenditure policies, 22

Galvin, Robert W., on national strategy needed for service sector, 78
Gilder, George
  on global economy, 51-52
  on U.S. dependence on Japanese technology, 35
Gorbachev, Mikhail, *glasnost* and *perestroika* and, 70, 71

Green, Robert T., on selective retaliation, 54
Gressner, Julian, on static interpretation of comparative advantage, 76

Hamilton, Alexander
  on policies to avoid dependence on foreign sources of essential supplies, 64
  on regulation of trade, 12
Hammer, Armand
  coal mine joint venture with People's Republic of China and, 93
  trade with USSR and, 69
Hawley, Willis, 48
Hofheinz, Roy, on Eastasian nationalism, 2
Hout, Thomas M., on industry affected by America's loss of competitive capability, 3
Huber, Peter W., on judgments in tort cases, 86
Huddle, Donald, on illegal aliens, 117

Jefferson, Thomas, on free trade, 64
Johnson, Chalmers
  on industrial policy, 44-45
  on two systems of political economy, 9
Johnson, Samuel, 1
Johnson, U. Alexis, on U.S. alliance with Japan, 27

Kasson, John A., on protectionism, 12
Kato, Hiroshi, on Japanese willingness to purchase more American assets, 34
Katsenelinboigen, Aron, on Mikhail Gorbachev's policies, 72
Kennedy, Paul M., on England's decline, 122-23
Keynes, John Maynard
  on favorable trade balance, 10
  on jobs, profits, and tariffs, 48-49
Kishimoti, Yoriko, on Western civilization, 118
Kotlin, Joel, on Western civilization, 118
Kramish, Arnold, on scientific attaches, 16
Kristol, Irving
  on corporations, 82
  on takeovers, 80

Kuznits, Paul W., on strategies in South Korea and Taiwan to advance their export-oriented industrial systems, 17

Larsen, Trina L., on selective retaliation, 54
Lenin, New Economic Policy of, 72
List, Friedrich
  on industrial policy, 76
  on mercantilism, 11-12
Lowenstein, Louis, on line between speculation and investment, 84

McConnell, Mitch, on liabilty system, 86
Malabre, Alfred L., Jr.
  on foreign capital in the U.S., 38
  on living standards and decline of the dollar, 61
Mises, Ludwig von, on goal of liberalism, 11
Morse, Ronald A., on significance of Japan for United States, 51, 53, 54
Mulkern, Louis, on role of government in the economy, 44

Nakasone, Yasuhiro, 34
Niskanen, William, on trade deficit, 56

Olson, Walter, on de-nationalization of financial power, 38-39

Perot, H. Ross
  on stock market reform, 84
  on takeovers, 81-82
  on U.S. national debt, 32
Perry, Matthew, 2
Peter the Great, Mikhail Gorbachev precedent set by, 71
Peterson, Peter O., on Japan's economic growth compared to America's, 7
Phillips, Kevin
  on industrial policy successes, 44
  on U.S. vulnerability, 124
Pierce, Neal, on takeovers, 82

NAME INDEX

Reagan, Ronald
  devaluation of the dollar and, 55
  recent change of policy and, 70
Rees, Albert, on unions' effect on economy, 108
Ricardo, David, on free trade, 10
Roberts, J.N., on Western civilization, 118
Roosevelt, Theodore, on protection of American producers, 13
Rostow, Walt W., on survival of American society, 1

Safire, William, on oil import fee, 93
Shultz, George, on new internationalism, 13
Simon, William E., on foreign funds borrowed to finance consumption, 32
Sinclair, Stuart, on trade and industrial policies, 43
Smith, Adam, on capacity to produce as source of power, 65
Smoot, Reed, 48
Stalin, Josef, 72
Stopler, Wolfgang F., on oil prices, 58
Swearingen, Robert, on Soviet investment in infrastructure and industry, 97

Taussig, Frank, on tariffs, 50
Taylor, Jared, on Japanese attitudes and investment and control, 7

Thirlwill, A.P., on harmful declines in manufacturing employment in advanced capitalist economies, 75
Timofeyev, Lev, on possible military dictatorship in USSR, 72
Trost, Carlisle A.H., on foreign-produced components of military and aerospace items, 67
Tucker, Jan, on global interdependence, 106

Verity, C. William, Jr., new avenues of trade with USSR and, 70

Wadbrook, William P., on vulnerability of United States, 67
Weinberger, Caspar, on U.S. and Soviet industrial bases, 66
Wilson, Charles, on mercantilism and international trade, 12
Wood, Christopher
  on electronic integration of financial markets, 53
  on market disturbances, 83

Zysman, John
  on global struggle for manufacturing technology, 76-77
  on military power depending on industrial capacity and technological innovation, 68

Index of Companies, Organizations and Institutions

American Economics Association, 57
American Immigration Control Foundation, 117
Armed Services Committee (U.S. House of Representatives), 64-65

Bank of Japan, 38
Barron's, 91
Boston University, 100
Brady Commission, 83
Business Week, 21

Chase Econometrics, 4
Claremont Economics Institute, 56
Columbia University (Center for Law and Economics), 84
Committee for Economic Development, 97
Council of Economic Advisors (CEA), 56, 73

Eastman Kodak Company, 17
The Economist, 39, 83
Electronic Data Systems, 32

Federal Emergency Management Agency, 67
Federal Reserve Board, 85
Federal Savings and Loan Insurance Corporation (FSLIC), 85
Florida International University, 106
Forbes, 35
Foreign Policy Research Institute, 72
Fujitsu, 79

Goldman Sachs, 38
Grace Commission, 24

Harvard University, 2
Hitachi, 79
Hormel Company, 111

IBM, 16
Inc., 118
Indiana University, 17
Industrial Bank of Japan, 38
Industry Week, 34
Institute for International Economics, 21
Intel, 16
Interagency National Acid Precipitation Program (U.S.), 102

Johns Hopkins University, 14
Joint Congressional Committee on Defense Production, 66
Joint Economic Committee, 3

Library of Congress, 51

Manhattan Foundation, 38-39
Manufacturers Hanover Trust, 7
Massachusetts Institute of Technology (MIT), 13, 16
Ministry of International Trade and Industry (MITI), 4, 79
Mobilization Concepts Development Center of National Defense University, 67
Motorola, 79

Mitsubishi, 79
Munitions Board, 96

National Association of Manufacturers, 22
National Aeronautics and Space Administration (NASA), 79
National Defense Stockpile (U.S.), 94
National Defense University, 67, 96
National Education Association (NEA), 105-106
National Journal, 82
National Labor Relations Board (NLRB), 109
National Security Council, 73-74, 96
National Security Resources Board, 96
NEC, 79
New York Governor's Advisory Committee on Insurance, 87
The New York Times, 93
North Atlantic Treaty Organization (NATO), 25, 26
Northwestern University, 57

Occidental Petroleum, 69, 93
Oil-Producing and Exporting Countries (OPEC), 91
Oki, 79
Orbis, 72
Oxford University (Merton College), 118

Pension Benefit Guarantee Corporation, 87
Pentagon, 24
Princeton University, 108

Republican Party, 12
Rice University, 117

Seabrook nuclear reactor (N.H.), 98
Shoreham nuclear plant (Long Island), 98
Social Security, 88
Sony, 41
Stanford University, 118
Strategic Petroleum Reserve, 95
Sumitomo Bank of Japan, 38
Sumitomo Group, 38

Teamster's Union, 107, 109
Tennessee Military Institute, 33
Toshiba Corporation, 37, 79
TRW, Inc., 37

United Nations, 43
U.S. International Trade Commission, 3
US-USSR Chamber of Commerce, 69
US-USSR Trade and Economic Council (USTEC), 69-70
University of California at Berkeley, 9, 68
University of Michigan, 58
University of Pennsylvania, 72
University of Southern California at Los Angeles, 38, 43, 97
University of Texas at Austin, 54

The Wall Street Journal, 38, 61, 80, 102
Wharton School (University of Pennsylvania), 72

Anthony Harrigan is president of the U.S. Industrial Council Educational Foundation. He is the author, co-author and editor of 17 books. His newspaper column appears in daily papers across the country, and his articles have been published in *The New York Times*, *National Review*, *Chronicles*, and other leading journals here and abroad. He has lectured on economic issues at colleges and universities nationwide, including Yale University, the University of Colorado, Virginia Military Institute, Pepperdine University, Clemson University and the U.S. Army War College.

William Hawkins is a consultant to the U.S. Business and Industrial Council and The South Foundation. He has taught economics at Radford University and the University of North Carolina at Asheville. He is a frequent contributor to *National Review*, *Chronicles*, *Strategic Review*, and other publications.